SPLENDOR
OF YOU®

Praise for THE SPLENDOR OF YOU®

"Don't listen to 'the world.' Listen to Deby. 'The world' tells us faith oppresses, smothers self-worth, and leads to guilt and neurosis. Deby tells us loving God brings peace, joy, and freedom, while affirming everything true, good, and beautiful within us. We are God's work of art. He looks at us and smiles. Thanks, Deby, for tenderly yet powerfully reminding us that - as Jesus whispered - in the end, it's all about love."

> —Timothy Michael Cardinal Dolan, Archbishop of New York

"Deby Schlapprizzi reveals the secret to every woman's success: her God-given dignity and talent. Through heartfelt personal reflections, she reminds every woman how to rediscover her splendor and transform her own life, as well as the society and culture at large, by sharing that splendor with the world. Her words are uplifting and inspiring, yet concrete and practical. A must-read for all women of faith!"

> —Susanna Pinto, Executive Producer, EWTN News Nightly

"This book changes lives. It touches the heart with stunning simplicity and stirs us in ways that we intuitively know to be true. Give it as a gift to every woman you know. St. Teresa of Avila, St. Catherine of Siena, and Pope St. John Paul II would all enthusiastically endorse this book."

> —Sister Regina Marie Gorman, O.C.D., Vicar General, Carmelite Sisters of the Most Sacred Heart of Los Angeles

"Deby Schlapprizzi's deep and steadfast Christian faith has daily opened her eyes to see the great beauty of her life in Christ, both in the joys and in the sorrows which are the fabric of every life. Over the years, she has helped other women to see more clearly the truth, goodness, and beauty of the gift of womanhood. What she has communicated in so many personal conversations and through the media, especially the radio, she now shares by her book, The Splendor of You™. As you come to know Deby through her book, may you come to know Christ and, thus, come to know the incomparable beauty of your life in Him."

> —Raymond Leo Cardinal Burke, Founder, Shrine of Our Lady of Guadalupe

"My friend, Deby, has a gift for encouraging others. She can see your strengths and struggles and help you on your journey with Christ to find the Splendor of You. You have it, let Deby help you discover it, and live it joyfully. Don't miss the balloons! This book is a treasure. As you read it, you will think of so many people you will want to share it with."

> —Teresa M. Holman, Co-Founder, Covenant Network Catholic Radio

"In these ponderings, Deby Schlapprizzi once again gifts us with her amazing insight, spiritual wisdom, practical wit, and deep personal prayer life. Her belief that "everything is already within you" is a testament to her faith in God's Grace - the driving force inside everyone whose heart desires God and His Love poured out on all peoples. With St. Irenaeus, Deby teaches that "the glory of God is a person fully alive!"

> —Sister Joseph Andrew Bogdanowicz, O.P., Co-Founder, Dominican Sisters of Mary, Mother of the Eucharist

"The Splendor of You® is an excellent example of what Pope St. John Paul II called the 'feminine genius.' Deby Sansone Schlapprizzi provides readers with inspirational meditations derived from her prayerful reflection on both the ordinary and extraordinary events of her own life. In the process, she gives thoughtful testimonies on the power of Catholic devotions such as the family rosary and Eucharistic Adoration. In addition to being great spiritual reading, The Splendor of You™ is a wonderful tool for personal prayer and meditation."
    —Joseph F. Naumann, D.D., Archbishop of Kansas City

"Nuggets of truth... Real-life stories... Words of wisdom. These are the 'gems' found in The Splendor of You™. With her down-to-earth style and inspiring faith, Deby has captured the heart of women and has given us a true gift. You won't want to put this book down!"
    —Patty Schneier, Catholic Speaker and Author

"In reading Deby's heartfelt words in this lovely and inspiring book, you will be looking into a truly humble and open heart! The Holy Spirit has been unleashed by her generous surrender to His power working in her. I pray that her words may touch you, her reader, in a way that brings you closer to His Merciful Love, in a special way during this Jubilee Year of Divine Mercy!"
    —Mother M. Angelina Finnell, Superior General, Carmelite Sisters of the Divine Heart of Jesus

"Deby Sansone Schlapprizzi has written a series of reflections for women whose message is acknowledging and then deeply coming to know the vision that God has for us. Deby uses the majestical word 'splendor' that describes what was instilled in us from the very beginning of time. She exhorts us to find our inner voice and to follow that voice, not the myriad voices that we're deluged with daily from outside of ourselves. As a psychologist, I have come to realize that this is the path to attaining both psychological and spiritual maturity."
    —Mary Fitzgibbons, Ph.D., Licensed Psychologist and Author

"Deby Schlapprizzi has tapped into the eternal Gospel message for all women that began with Eve and ended with Blessed Mary, the Mother of God – women were created by a magnificent God to bring about His Plan for humanity that encompasses Love, Joy, and Trust. When we women partake in this 'Intimacy with God,' we discover true 'Splendor.' Thank you, Deby, for this gift from God."
    —Ann G. Martin, M.D., Associate Professor of Medicine, Washington University
      in St. Louis

The
SPLENDOR
of YOU®

33 REFLECTIONS

TO DISCOVER THE LIGHT WITHIN

DEBY SANSONE SCHLAPPRIZZI

✝

SPLENDOR OF YOU® COMMUNICATIONS

FIRST EDITION

ISBN 978-0-9975837-0-0
51495

Published By
Splendor of You® Communications

For inquiries visit www.splendorofyou.com

Printed in U.S.A.

Book Cover Design by John Caruso
Interior Book Design by Jim Harper
Production Consultant, Margaret Fortner

THIS BOOK IS DEDICATED TO
— OUR LORD AND HIS MOTHER —
WHO PLACED IN MY HEART THE MESSAGE OF
THE SPLENDOR OF YOU THOSE MANY YEARS AGO.

"All of them differ, one from another, yet none of them has He made in vain.

For each, in turn, as it comes, is good; can one ever see enough of their splendor?"

— Sirach 42:25

TABLE OF CONTENTS

The
SPLENDOR
of YOU®

Foreword

· ·

Deby Sansone Schlapprizzi has been given a gift, a jewel that speaks of truth, beauty, and goodness… she calls it splendor. In simply compelling words this book gives a glimpse of the grandeur of God resident within you. Deby's insights, stories, and personal revelations allow you to find your own personal treasure and discover the "who" you truly are. This book captivates me, as I believe it will captivate you, too.

I first met Deby when she attended a talk I gave at the Archdiocese of St. Louis, however, it wasn't until she asked me as a guest on her Catholic radio program, "The Splendor of You®," that I realized how God has blessed her with such deep and practical wisdom, insight, and transcendence, as well as an empathetic and inspirational heart. I came to understand then that Deby must share her gift with others.

This book offers a double blessing. First, the book is so well-written, heartfelt, and personal that it causes you to nod in agreement and smile with gratitude… the very words seem to sparkle with grace. Second, the author so artfully describes the magnificence that God has planted in you — your individual splendor — that you find yourself immersed in deeper personal meaning and there discover new significance in your life.

Deby's spiritual personality, her splendor, shines through every page: her deep faith and God-reliance inspire you, her selflessness motivates you to look inside for what needs change, and her light illuminates new meaning onto how you imagine and interpret your walk with Jesus. She does all this with a compassionate heart and tender touch as she deftly calls you to a higher realm, a truer reality, a "place" where you can almost taste and see your true self… your unique splendor.

The author shows you that her feet are firmly planted on the ground; she's familiar with the world, but certainly not worldly. Looking through Deby's eyes you can see your life differently; she elevates your vision so you see your "every-dayness" as pregnant with significance, not mundane but magnificent. Her words give you pause to reconnect with the pulse of the Spirit within you, re-member your often fragmented spirit, and re-inspire your sometimes deflated soul with a compelling, "common sense" vision of the joy of following Christ.

The book lets you relax in grace and just "be" your true self, instead of contorting yourself in the press of going here and doing that. Deby gives you a new yardstick so you can measure the days of your life with the spiritual metric of God's truth, and not devalue yourself by using the lifeless yardstick of the world.

Deby's words are more than simple; they are simply beautiful… even profound. Her words caused me to repeatedly look-up from my reading and allow them to seep into my heart and soul — I wanted to behold them, not just observe them, and to embrace them, not merely greet them. After you read her book through, you'll want to keep it close at hand to re-open it whenever the Spirit strikes, so you can re-imagine her words, take them in again, and find a new nuance of peace, hope, and love that you may have missed before.

You may find it a bit strange that a man is writing the Foreword to this book when it is clearly written for women and from a woman's perspective. As a psychologist, I've worked with thousands of women particularly in areas of transition, wellness, and spiritual development. I've also learned deeply about commitment, togetherness, and intimacy from over 30 years of marriage counseling. Deby's words remind me that the beauty of the feminine is in each of us regardless of our earthly gender. This book affirms my love for the Blessed Mother and for my wife. So, while this book is primarily written for women, I recommend it for men as well in the hope that it can give them the same gifts it has given me.

Richard P. Johnson, Ph.D.

Dr. Johnson is an author of more than 40 books including: The 12 Keys to Spiritual Vitality, Body-Mind-Spirit, Loving for a Lifetime, The Power of Smiling, Discover Your Spiritual Strengths, Healing Wisdom, Because I Care, and others. He is a sought-after speaker having given many presentations, including keynote addresses at major Catholic organizations. Dr. Johnson was awarded an honorary doctorate (beyond his earned doctorate) by Holy Cross College, at Notre Dame, for his work in spiritual gerontology. He is an active counselor specializing in "spiritual personality dynamics" through the JOHNSON Institute (www. SeniorAdultMinistry.com). Dr. Johnson is also the creator of the Spiritual Strengths Profile. (Discover your spiritual personality www.SpiritualStrengthsProfile.com.)

Introduction

It is not by happenstance that you've come upon this book. It is written with you in mind; for every woman that was, is, and will be.

This work is about you and the magnificence of God's splendor that lives within you. It's your companion for the journey, a guide, and a reminder of the treasure that is rightfully yours.

As women, we often abandon our true selves. We recognize gifts in others, but seldom in ourselves. Even worse, we abandon the vision God has for us. All that you will be is not yet known, yet the pinnacle of who you are already exists, for God wanted you from the beginning of time.

The Lord's will for you is to be whole and complete — fully realized. And yet, at times, you may feel like you're just getting by. Some of us have never known how to be fully ourselves, and others among us may simply be worn out. Many of us may avoid thinking about the questions or doubts, or we may be afraid to pray for God's will. I've been there myself. I've been afraid He will hurt or disappoint me and those I love.

And yet the truth is that it is only through His will that we receive peace. It is only through His will that we find our true selves — that we discover joy and freedom. No one knows more about you and me than Jesus. No one knows more about your heartaches and joys than Jesus. No one loves you more than He does, and no one wants you to be more complete and whole than the Lord. He holds the key.

Your job is to be you and my job is to be me — to be perfectly ourselves. It's not an easy task in a world of comparison, woundedness, and perfectionism. The gifts you have are different than mine and mine are different than yours. And that's okay because we were created this way. It's not only okay, it's a gift; a magnificent gift of splendor to be celebrated, savored, and shared.

There is no right or wrong way to read *The Splendor of You*®. Wherever you are right now, whoever you are, just begin. Each reflection is meant to help you recognize and experience a renewed sense of your splendor, your purpose, and God's matchless love for you.

Any suggestions in this book are my simple and humble attempts to provide you with steadying handholds along the way. Everything you need is already within you — the Lord dwells within you and you can meet Him always. But that very same Lord also calls us to help one another, and my prayer is that the reflections in this book will do just that — help you to shine even brighter.

Whatever your age, your state in life, or your circumstances, think of Christ saying to you, *"You are My gift to the world. You have a splendor that the world longs to see…a light on a hill."*

It's time — perhaps past time — to embrace the vision God has for you. It's time to enjoy your birthright as the Daughter of the King, and to experience the hope and blessing of all you were created to be.

Welcome to the wonder and the beauty of
The Splendor Of You.

Splendor = who you are
+ the promise you *hold*

Splendor =
who you are +
the promise
you Hold

Reflection ❶

Seeing Your Splendor

> *"For a very long time I considered low self-esteem to be some kind of virtue. I had been warned so often against pride and conceit that I came to consider it a good thing to deprecate myself. But now I realize that the real sin is to deny God's first love for me, to deny my original goodness. Because without claiming that first love and that original goodness for myself, I lose touch with my true self and embark on the destructive search among the wrong people and in the wrong places for what can only be found in the house of my Father."*
> — **Henri Nouwen, *The Return of the Prodigal Son***

More than 2,000 years ago, an archangel left the house of the Father to visit a young Jewish girl, proclaiming to her: ***"You who are highly favored! The Lord is with you."*** With her simple 'yes,' the maiden was transformed from an unknown village girl to Queen of the Universe. She is Mary — Woman of Splendor.

Like Mary, you, too, are called to hear the Father's words that you are ***"highly favored."*** You, too, are invited to embrace and live your splendor.

What do I mean when I say "splendor"? Splendor is the "divine DNA" of who you are — your singular temperament, personality, gifts, capacity for love, as well as the promise you hold. Your splendor is the Father's unique design for you and you alone.

3

When I was in the midst of a personal struggle years ago, a dear friend and Carmelite sister, Sr. Regina Marie, said to me:

"You are a good idea — God's idea. If you weren't, He would have skipped over you and gone on to another, but He didn't; He came up with you!"

Splendor is just that — God's idea. There is no one like you, no one who can be the you that He has created. He sees something in you that you may not see.

Even Scripture tells us that we can never see enough of our splendor. Made in God's image and likeness, each of us has immeasurable value and promise which comes alive when we respond to God's invitation to become all He has created us to be.

So I ask you…

Do you shortchange the gifts you've been given?
Do you shortchange yourself?

Do you find excuses to leave your splendor buried and dormant?

Have you gotten used to accepting the counterfeit rather than the authentic?

Do you hide behind fear or confusion?

Has sin gotten a foothold without you even noticing?

Do you play the blame game where the only loser is you?

And what will you do about it? The choice is yours.

Will you…

Settle for less? *Stay* stuck? *Be* indifferent? *Remain* bitter?

Be a victim? *Get* frustrated? *Run* away? *Remain* afraid?

Get lost in the rush and frenzy and false obligation?

And, in the process, will you abandon your splendor?

Or will you

Persevere in *hope* and *prayer*?

Dare to dream big dreams,
even if you've been disappointed?

Many of us get stuck in a false image of who we are and the illusion
that we're not good enough. But we must claim our original goodness.
This original goodness — *your truest self* — is your splendor.

Today, I invite you to ask your Father in heaven what splendor exists within
you that has yet to shine. Reach for the hand of Our Lady as you begin this
journey. Mary lived her splendor perfectly and will help you to go further, dig
deeper, and begin to see your own. Now is a good time to invite her to walk
this road with you.

Lord,
please give me the grace
to believe in You
and Your goodness.
Please open the eyes of my soul to see as You see.
May I begin to see my splendor.
O Lord, please give me the grace
to realize that You love me...
that I am beautifully and wonderfully made.
You know me.
You gave me my personality, my gifts, my heart.
Help me to not let the world crowd You out.
Please give me the grace to know who I am.
I'm ready, Lord.
Help me to become all that You created me to be and to know
that it's never too late.
I love You, Lord.
I rely on You, Jesus.
I thank You for giving me Your Mother as my guide on this
journey —
the Queen of Hope, the Model of Splendor.
Amen.

making the most
of one's best.

"One must have the adventurous

daring to accept oneself as a bundle of possibilities and undertake the most interesting game in the world — making the most of one's best."

— Harry Emerson Fosdick

Reflection ❷

Becoming a Masterpiece

> *"I am confident of this, that the one who began a good work in you will continue to complete it until the day of Christ Jesus." — Philippians 1:6*

*H*ave you ever had the privilege of seeing Michelangelo's David in person? If so, you know what an extraordinary work it is. I'll never forget when I first walked into the Accademia Museum in Florence, Italy, eagerly anticipating the sight, and there he was — an awe-inspiring form! Loud voices hushed to reverent whispers as visitors around me approached the renowned sculpture.

For Michelangelo, the task of the sculptor was to free the splendor already contained within the stone, to remove all that was "not David." Think about that — even before the first strike of the chisel, David, in his magnificence, was already there.

It's like that with you and me as well — our splendor is already within us, waiting to be fully revealed! You're invited by God, with the help of His grace, to chisel away all that isn't your true self so that you're eventually left with the masterpiece God made you to be.

You are a David.

We are all Davids —

God's magnificient masterpieces!

Magnificence exists regardless of age, health, abilities, or circumstances. Your magnificence, your splendor, is much like God's love. You have it whether you feel it, accept it, see it, sabotage it, or even ignore it — your splendor is just there. The task for each of us is to free what is carried within, to continually chip away at anything that detracts from our splendor. It is a gem within you that is as unique as your fingerprint.

Don't allow yourself to get discouraged. This journey takes time and you won't arrive immediately. David's splendor didn't emerge from the stone in one strike of the hammer to the chisel. Likewise, each of us gets there step by step, moment by moment. If you're unsure how or what this looks like or how to get there, don't worry; the realization, the understanding, will come — you'll see. Be patient and trust that you're being led.

At times, I have to be reminded that I'm not alone in this journey. And you are not alone either. No matter how you feel, you aren't alone. All of heaven is at your beck and call — an unseen world surrounds you.

Today, ask God to help you begin chiseling away at all that is not authentically you and call upon all of heaven to accompany you on this journey. Consider using the words of St. Anselm: *"Acknowledge in Your goodness what is Your own in me and what is not Your own, wipe off from me."*

My Lord, You know who I am —
who I truly am.
Please give me the grace to become the person
You have created me to be.
Protect me from discouragement.
Keep me from growing impatient with myself and others.
Let me know that I am Your masterpiece.
Please remove all that is not the true _____(place your name).
I trust in Your timing, Lord, and Your patience with me.
Soften my ways, open my heart, temper my desire for instant
answers and control.
Fill me with Your confidence.
Please give me a fuller realization of my purpose, my worth,
my dignity, my splendor.
I ask this in Jesus' name in the company of
Our Lady and all the angels and saints.
Amen.

"Spirit of the Living God

fall afresh on me...
melt me,
mold me,
fill me,
use me."

— From "Spirit of the
Living God Fall Afresh on Me"

Reflection ❸

More Than a Feeling

> *"We know that in everything God works for good with those who love him, who are called according to his purpose." — Romans 8:28*

Not long ago, a close friend of mine named Karen lost her beloved husband after a lengthy illness. She told me that within an hour of his passing — "after a really deep sob" — she felt nothing but joy, realizing he was reunified with his loved ones. Even in the midst of her deep sorrow, Karen experienced the hand of God on her life and the promise He makes to all of us that we are not alone and death is not the end.

A few months later I visited Karen with my beloved friend, Pat, and frankly, we were blown away. Karen was living alone in a new community in a new city and although she was still suffering, she had a peace and strength that was palpable and inspiring. We visited with the hope of lifting her spirits and instead, the reverse happened. Karen blessed us through her faith, her trust — and her cross. Her splendor was not diminished in her heartache; if anything, it shone even brighter.

Discovering and living our splendor is not to be mistaken with "feeling good." It's not about being upbeat all the time and having no pain or suffering. True happiness isn't about circumstances; it's about intimacy with our Lord. Intimacy with Him is about total connectedness with the One who fully and completely accepts and loves us.

How do we enjoy this kind of intimacy with God in order to live in true joy and not at the whim of passing emotions? The answer is simpler than you may think.

One day in prayer while reading the scriptures I came upon the story of Mary Magdalene and the empty tomb. She searched for Jesus — worried, confused, desperate, not seeing Him, not finding Him. And yet He was standing right beside her, she just didn't recognize Him. I thought to myself, I'm like Mary Magdalene; we're all Mary Magdalenes. We search for the Lord and yet He's beside us all the time.

Even if it feels like Jesus is far away, He is with you. Do not grow weary of bringing yourself to prayer again and again and reminding yourself of this, regardless of how you may feel. Prayer is the key to living in a place of peace and joy and letting your splendor shine, no matter what your emotional state may be.

Today, be aware of what feelings come and go, and at the same time remind yourself throughout the day that Jesus is right beside you, and that your true joy and peace lie in Him.

My Lord and my God,
there are going to be "days"
on this side of heaven –
tough moments and up and down emotions,
challenging seasons of life,
and heartache.
Help me to step back, take a breath, and look closer.
The truth is that You are with me . . . always . . .
carrying me through the ins and outs of my life.
Place Your healing, steady hand on me.
Lord Jesus. I rest in You.
Use the circumstances of my life
to allow my splendor to shine forth.
Jesus, I trust in You.
May Your most perfect will be mine.
Give me the strength to carry on.
Amen

"*I always thought that* if a calling was from God, or if I'm good enough, everything would simply fall into place...it ought to be fairly easy, it ought to just work...doors should open left and right and opportunities abound. Upon sharing my 'keen insight' with a reputable counselor his first question was, 'who in the world ever told you that?!', I remember responding...hm-mmmm...I think I came up with that myself."

—Deby

Reflection 4

···

Living Big

> *"For I know well the plans I have in mind for you… plans for your*
> *welfare and not for woe, so as to give you a future of hope."*
> *— Jeremiah 29:11*

All too often we women "play it small." What does this mean? It means
that we settle for less, for the mediocre, and that we allow our fears or
disappointments to dictate our actions and decisions. Many of us operate
out of our fears and uncertainty rather than our hopes and dreams. When
did we trade in our inner voice? When did fear and trepidation become our
compass? You and I are called to something bigger.

A few years ago, my daughter, Annie, faced a major career decision. In a
difficult job market she was offered a reputable and reliable job near her
Midwestern hometown — one that didn't excite or draw her. Many of her
advisors encouraged her to take the job. "You need this job," they told her,
"take it!" She was torn between what her inner voice was telling her and the
pressure she felt to do what looked obvious and rational to outsiders.

In the midst of her dilemma, Annie was reminded of the wise words a
holy priest gave to her many years before, spoken in his Italian accent:
"Sometimes, you need to go against the 'streaming.'"

It was time for my daughter to step back, sit with it, and ask herself: How do I really feel? Does this job light me up? Does it bring me joy?

After some deliberation and prayer, Annie turned down the offer. She realized God was asking her to trust Him and reach far, not play it safe. She was being invited to look into her heart and see what she was being called to do. She trusted and God took care of the rest. The answers didn't come easily, but with prayer and perseverance remarkable opportunities opened up for Annie — the kind that only happen when you let God take the reins.

You see, Annie received a call from God to trust, to pay attention to her inner voice, to not settle — and that involved some risk. But she was worth more than playing it safe. We all are.

God doesn't want any of us to live small, or to settle for less in any area of our lives. He calls us to live big. Living big is about courage, perseverance, and honoring your inner voice. It's about spending time in daily prayer and asking the questions: What brings me joy? What lights me up? When am I fully alive? As you answer these questions, you begin to recognize your splendor.

The Lord has a specific plan for you and His plan is never stagnant — it will take you somewhere, and challenge you to grow and change. Don't be afraid of that; God is beside you. Be patient. When you live in His constantly evolving plan, you discover your splendor. This splendor blossoms in every season of your life and has no beginning and no end … there's no retirement from your splendor.

Today, ask yourself: Are you settling for mediocrity? Are you settling in your relationships or with your dreams? Are you settling when it comes to your talents? Perhaps you've never asked these questions. Consider asking them now. Maybe you, too, are called to "go against the 'streaming.'"

Make the decision to stop living small and settling for less. Ask the Lord to give you the courage to start living bigger and bolder. Ask Him to carry you through your fears and uncertainties. Ask Him to show you where to begin. Remember, small steps lead to greater ones — so take a small step today.

Lord Jesus, You created me,
conceived of me before the world began.
Please open my mind, my heart,
my life to the plans You have for me . . .
I repent of living small.
Remove fear and trepidation from my life.
Help me to live bigger, each day.
Help me to know what that means for me.
Please, Lord, take over my life.
Lead me.
Give me the grace to become all
You have created me to be.
Amen.

"...When you walk through

a storm hold your head up high. And don't be afraid of the dark. At the end of a storm is a golden sky and the sweet silver song of a lark."

— "You'll Never Walk Alone" by Elvis Presley, written by Rogers and Hammerstein

Reflection ⑤
....

The Lesson of Naomi

"Behold, I make all things new." — Revelation 21:5

*J*esus says to each and every one of us: *"Behold, I make all things new."* Perhaps there are times when you think that the Lord makes things new for other people, but not for you. Maybe you've been waiting and waiting and have asked repeatedly for newness in your life and then, nothing. But remember, God says He makes all things new.

I was feeling that way when I came across a TV evangelist who was sharing the life-giving story of Naomi from the Book of Ruth. It's a story that has been shared by evangelists, preachers, and priests everywhere for good reason — it's a powerful example of the promise God makes to us.

Naomi's life was good and she was happy. She loved her husband and their two sons. But one day heartbreak arrived on Naomi's doorstep; her beloved husband died. Following his death, her sons took wives — Orpah and Ruth — and they all lived together for ten years. Naomi loved her family, but when her beloved sons died deep sadness set in once again.

Naomi decided to return to Bethlehem, and told Ruth and Orpah to return to their mothers. But Ruth repeatedly refused to leave Naomi, giving us one of the most inspirational quotes of the Old Testament: *"Wherever you go I will go, and wherever you lodge I will lodge. Your people shall be my people and your God, my God. Where you die I will die, and there be buried"* (Ruth 1:16-17).

So together, Naomi and her devoted daughter-in-law, Ruth, moved to Bethlehem.

The first chapter of Ruth tells us:
On their arrival, the whole town was excited about them, and the women asked: "Can this be Naomi?" But she said to them, "Do not call me Naomi. Call me Mara, for the Almighty has made my life very bitter. I went away full, but the Lord has brought me back empty (19-21).

But God wasn't finished with Naomi. There were to be more seasons of fulfillment and joy for her — even through the suffering and loss. While in Bethlehem, Ruth meets a man named Boaz, a powerful relative of Naomi and owner of a grain field in which Ruth works. Boaz falls in love with Ruth and marries her, and she bears a son named Obed.

Then the women said to Naomi,
"Blessed is the Lord who has not failed to provide you today with a redeemer. May he become famous in Israel! He will restore your life and be the support of your old age, for his mother is the daughter-in-law who loves you. She is worth more to you than seven sons!" Naomi took the boy, cradled him against her breast, and cared for him (Ruth 4:14-16).

Of course, Naomi's grandson was no ordinary child. Obed became the father of Jesse, who had a son named David — King David. David was the second king of Israel, heir to the royal line, and ancestor of Jesus Christ.

Naomi, who had given up on life, who thought God had betrayed her, who had even changed her name from Naomi (which means pleasant, delightful, and lovely) to Mara (which means bitter), was blessed with a new season; one she hadn't planned or imagined, yet one that fulfilled her beyond her expectations.

Naomi could have said, "I'm too old." But God says, You're just the right age for my plan for you.

Naomi could have said, "I have no hope." But God says, Believe… have faith — I make all things new. You are my masterpiece.

Naomi could have said, "But God, I was bitter and angry with you, and I made mistakes. I forgot about you." But God says, I forgive you. I love you. I've been here all along.

What is your sadness? Where do you feel hopeless? Life isn't over — there are more seasons. You're here right now; you're alive! Your future, no matter your age or circumstance, can be blessed. You may know loss and emptiness as Naomi did, but just as that didn't stop a new season in her life, it doesn't have to stop one in yours.

Today, invite Jesus into this moment. Ask Him to help you live the life He created for you since the beginning of time. Ask Him to help you see with eyes of faith, to see with His eyes and experience His peace. No matter the hardship and pain you've experienced or are presently experiencing, ask our Lord to give you a "new season" of healing, wisdom, love, and gratitude. Prayer and doing the next right thing gives us the grace to move on and live a new season.

Lord Jesus please help me to have hope,
to believe in a "new season" for my life.
Please my Lord, rescue me from my distress.
Sometimes I see no way out.
I rely on You to remind me of who I am; that I am loved by You.
I rely on You to remind me that I'm Your daughter.
I rely on You to pick me up, brush me off, and carry me to the new season of
life You have created me for.
I trust in Your words "Behold I make all things new,"
not just for some, but for all — for me.
I'm ready, Lord.
Please have mercy.
I ask for a new season of healing,
wisdom and love, and a new season
of splendor to come forth.
I love You, my Lord.
Please give me the grace to
never turn my back on You.
Amen.

Call to *Me*

"Call to *Me* and I will ANSWER and tell you great and unsearchable things you do not know!"

–Jeremiah 33:3

Reflection ⑥

....

> *The word of the Lord came to Jeremiah not in a loud thunderous*
> *voice, but in a still, small voice.*
> —*a paraphrase of 1 Kings 19: 11-12*

*Y*ears ago, my husband Don and I took a trip which we hoped would be a wonderful and relaxing experience. Instead, it was stressful, with arbitrary deadlines and obligations. I remember thinking, Whoa! Something's wrong with this picture! After some thought and prayer, we stepped back and began slowing down. We listened to our inner voice, acknowledged what was and wasn't working, and started to follow our own rhythm. As a result, the trip was transformed. It was an eye-opener.

So often we live rushed, frenzied lives, tumbling from one situation to the next — barely breathing through it all. But if we can listen to that still, small voice within us it makes all the difference. That voice is often the Holy Spirit speaking, pointing us in the direction that will lead us closer to God and to our authentic selves — to our splendor.

It can be difficult to step back and listen to that voice within, especially when you feel pressure from others, from your own ego, or when life's busyness and confusion crowd it out. But when you do, you are better able to make the choices that help you stay true to yourself and grow in your splendor — which leads to a more joy-filled life.

Your inner voice has wisdom. It knows what lifts your spirit and draws your heart, which are clues to the way God invites you to live your splendor. You can't hear your inner voice unless you force yourself to be still and listen — to quiet down. It requires courage and letting go, because sometimes following your inner voice means speaking up for yourself or someone else, or choosing a different path.

Through prayer you can learn to recognize that still, small voice — the Holy Spirit's promptings within you. And when you do, it blesses others because they feel permission to follow a more authentic way for themselves. This is true for all of us, that when we witness authenticity modeled in someone else, a shift can take place inside us and we can see there's another way of living, one that's in greater harmony with who God has created us to be.

What if you hear nothing when you stop and listen to the Holy Spirit? Hearing only silence is still hearing. It's active. Sometimes in prayer there is silence. So be silent; sit with it.

Imagine a mother holding her newborn baby; does she constantly speak to her child? Often, she just rocks that baby in silence. Silence isn't a punishment, rather, it's a language of love all its own. Don't be dismayed or agitated if you experience silence with Christ, as that, too, is His voice, His whisper. Let Him hold you in the quiet and be at peace.

The fact is, each of us needs these moments throughout the day when we step aside, get quiet, and slow down in order to be fully alive and at peace. So today, take a few minutes in prayer to listen for that inner voice, and ask the Lord to help you tune into that voice every day, and to follow it.

Lord Jesus, please give me the grace to know that You speak to me.
Please silence the chatter within.
Give me the grace to listen to Your whisper and the patience
to wait on Your word.
Please stop the merry-go-round of my life
so that I live purposefully and intentionally with my eyes wide open.
I love You. I trust You.
Please lead me to the life You call me to live.
May I be present to Your word, and hear Your voice.
Amen.

"*Everyone*

has his own fingerprints.

The white light streams down to be broken up by those human prisms into all the colors of the rainbow.

Take your own color in the pattern &

be just that."

– Charles R. Brown

Reflection ❼

....

Stepping Out

> *Do not be afraid. Do not be satisfied with mediocrity. Put out*
> *into the deep and let down your nets for a catch.*
> *– Pope Saint John Paul II*

*H*ave you ever been scared, really scared to step out and do something? Where you faced a choice between discontentment and the possibility of "something more"?

We all have those moments in our lives — defining moments, possible turning points that can bring us into a new and wider horizon.

I had such a moment. It came a few years ago when I was speaking at a national women's conference. Leading up to it I found myself wanting "more" and aware that my trail of excuses and justifications had come to an end.

I had spoken to many audiences over the years. Early on, most of my speaking was directed to high school teens under the umbrella of chastity. This time was different: I'd be sharing this new message about splendor for the first time — with over 1,000 women of all ages and various backgrounds. It was an opportunity to step into a deeper, richer, fuller presentation of the concept of splendor. I was older now, and out of my comfort zone. Would I be good enough? Would they like me?

My anxiety only grew worse after I arrived. As I waited for my turn at the podium, a well-respected, widely known speaker was addressing the audience. The "you're-not-good-enough" script began playing over and over in my mind: *My remarks aren't like that. I'm making myself too vulnerable. Why did I choose such an emotional topic? What am I doing here?*

Then the words of my message came to mind: *You are beautifully and wonderfully made. You are singular and matchless. You are created in the image and likeness of God. I said to myself, God made me, me…I need to be me. Don't compare! I am wonderfully and beautifully made.*

The speaker concluded and music began to play as I was ushered to the stage. As I was being introduced I prayed, Lord, help me. Take over. I had prepared and I had sought the counsel of experts — at this point there was nothing more to do; God would have to carry me the rest of the way. Then I heard the lyrics of the intro song "My Grace Is Enough" and the minute I heard the words, a transition occurred; I suddenly knew He really was big enough to take over.

After I stood at the podium for a few moments, I suddenly felt compelled to get out from behind it. My kids later told me that when I stepped out, there was a shift, something powerful happened and the energy in the room changed. All I knew in the moment was that I had to be where I could share my heart and be me — not knowing if being me would be good enough. It was as if I was coming out of hiding… stepping out after holding back.

Even in the middle of my talk, I had no idea how it was going. When the audience applauded at different times, I didn't want to soak it up — in the past, I had "performed" too much as a speaker and was too concerned about the audience's perception of me. This time I wanted to stay focused on the message — the beauty of God's call to live our splendor.

When I finished, the incredibly generous audience rose in a standing ovation, and my husband stood there with thumbs up. Afterwards my daughter, Toni, rushed up to me wide-eyed, saying "Mom! Your CDs sold out! Everyone is asking for more!" I was shocked. Later that evening, it occurred to me that God was not only giving me permission to be myself, but calling me, summoning me to be myself.

Upon reflection, I realized that something powerful had happened to me at that conference: I had finally stepped out and answered God's call — His summons — to be myself. And being myself was more than good enough. Prior to this, I could see the splendor in other people, but I struggled to see it in myself. That day, I saw myself through God's eyes — and it was an epiphany.

What about you?

Do you have areas of discontentment in your life? If so, thank God for them; they're signals flagging you to step into something more. There's always a temptation to avoid stepping out; there are fears, doubts, and questions. Who knows what will happen if I do this? Maybe this is all there is! Maybe I'm being selfish. Maybe I want too much. But these are ploys to keep you from experiencing the life-giving transformation to which God calls you.

You have your own story, and stepping out to live your splendor will look different than someone else's path. Begin with silence. Pray. Be present to your longings and jot them down. Turn a deaf ear to the negative voices that belittle you. Pray some more. And if you need to seek counsel from a wise priest, minister, advisor, or friend — do it. Remember, God created us to help and be helped by one another. As a holy priest once said to me, "We need someone with skin on them."

Today, prayerfully consider where you need to step out. Then ask for the Lord's help and do it.

Father God, I praise You and give You glory.
You know my inner struggles and my fears.
Lead me.
Show me where You call me to step out, to break down the walls.
Please give me the grace to transform my life.
You are my shelter and my light.
I rely completely on You.
Give me the hope that comes only from
You and help me experience Your joy.
Let me begin to discover splendor, the splendor of me.
I pray to be fully realized — whole and complete.
Lord, I lean on You, trusting that
You will provide those who can help me.
Grant me the courage to follow through.
Amen.

there is always the
TEMPTATION

"*Sadly, there is always the*

TEMPTATION
to become lukewarm, to quench the
spirit, to refuse to invest the talents
we received for our own good and the
good of others."

(cf. Mt 25:25 ff)
– Pope Benedict XVI 2012
Lenten Message

Reflection ⑧

....

Discovering Your Talents

> *I am confident of this, that the one who began a good work in you will be*
> *faithful to complete it until the end of the day in Christ Jesus.*
> *— Philippians 1:6*

*D*o you know your talents — those specific gifts you've been endowed with — and how God may be calling you to use them? To live your splendor is to recognize and allow your God-given talents to shine.

Many of us don't acknowledge our talents — or we downplay them. We may lack the confidence to use our talents or be afraid of what using them will mean. But when we withhold our talents from the world, we live too small. God calls us to step out and be who He created us to be — and a big part of that is the way He has gifted us.

My daughter, Toni, reminded me of this one day. She was reading Father Jacques Philippe's *Searching for and Maintaining Peace*, and had accompanied me to an out-of-town speaking engagement. The night before my presentation I was struggling with some aspects of my talk. In the midst of my angst, she looked up at me and said, "You know mom, I read in Father's book that faith is like a parachute. First, you have to jump, and for a few moments there's that sense of nothing, you are alone, but then — the pull, the lifting up — the parachute grabs, opens, and you're soaring. Jesus is going to grab hold of you just like the cords of the parachute."

I had to jump, take action, go with my presentation, and trust.

Sometimes using our talents is just like that — jumping, even when we're afraid and wavering. There will be no soaring until we do. God calls us to act. It's not about waiting until you think you're good enough, or smart enough, or ready. If that were the case, none of us would do anything. It isn't even about whether you've identified all of your unique talents. It's about faith — trusting in the Lord's power, as well as your willingness to say "Yes! Yes, I have talents, given by God. I am valuable; I am called to use my gifts in this world." As a dear friend once pointed out to me, the Holy Spirit will fill the gaps between our limitations and the abundance of what is needed — He just needs our "yes."

As you go about your day, notice what you love, what resonates, what brings you and others joy. Ask those who know you, the people you trust — perhaps your spouse, a close friend, a sibling, older children, nieces and nephews: "What do you think I excel at naturally? Where have I been blessed? What am I doing when I am most happy?

I invite you to bring a journal to your prayer time and ask the Lord to help make your talents clear. Listen deeply and write what comes to you in the quiet of your soul. There's no need for anxiety or discouragement and no "right" way. Rather, be at peace knowing you will discover your God-given talents gradually, step by step.

Be aware of your naysayer voice — the one that whispers I can't do that; I don't have that gift. It's too late. I'm too busy. This is too hard, I'll never come up with anything. Remember, God is a God of surprise. He is with you. Once you've identified your talents, you're called to develop them. Do you have the gift of compassion? Reach out to someone. Humor? Encourage another to laugh. Hospitality? Invite someone over.

Is it time for you to jump, to act, to use your gifts in a bigger fuller way? Today, Ask Jesus to show you your talents and to grant you the courage and grace to use them.

Lord, please make clear to me the gifts I possess
and the gifts I've buried.
Help me to believe that I possess a treasure, a brilliance,
a splendor that is only mine.
May I see my gifts and talents and use them to serve You.
I am Your gift to the world.
No one can do what You have created me to do.
Help me to discover what that is and give me the courage to do it.
Please remove any negativity and discouragement and
replace it with Your blessed truth.
Please remove whatever has stopped me in the past.
I love You, Lord.
Amen.

* A tool I have found very helpful for identifying my talents is the Spiritual Strengths Profile. You can find more about it in my Resource page at the end of this book.

"FOR WE ARE *his Handiwork* created in Christ Jesus for the good works that God has prepared in advance that we should live in them."

– Ephesians 2:10

Reflection ❾

....

The Call to Courage

> *"Our doubts are traitors, and make us lose the good we oft might win by fearing to attempt." — Shakespeare*

A few years ago my sister Cindy, a woman of many talents, felt called to do something new but didn't know what that "something" was. She began praying about the next step, listening to her inner voice, and sharing her feelings with family and trusted friends.

Soon, Cindy became aware of a calling to the fitness industry. At the same time she had a growing family and a demanding schedule in another professional field. Doubts started creeping in and she questioned her capabilities. She had attempted to break into the industry before, but didn't find a fit. Would this time be any different?

In the quiet of prayer, she was reminded of our dad's familiar words often repeated to us in our youth: "Look in your own back yard for your goldmine." With continued prayer and soul searching, the Lord opened her eyes to see what was under her nose: She already had the necessary space with a separate entrance to build an in-home fitness studio. So she took the plunge and opened her own business. It was not without risk and her fair share of doubts. What if no one showed? What if she ended up embarrassed? What if this was just a waste of money and prelude to disappointment?

Fast forward to today: If you go over to Cindy's studio any morning of the week, you'll find women of every fitness level working out side-by-side in an energized, supportive space — women caring for one another, networking, embracing life. What came out of this was much more than a business. A rosary hangs from a StairMaster® as an invitation and a reminder of the early days. Cindy is the first one to say that God made it all happen.

"When I was ready to call it quits, a phone call came through — another group to train. I persevered," she says.

Cindy now has a business with a waiting list that has tripled over the last three years. Even more, my sister's life has opened up in many wonderful ways and she has a keen sense of herself and her splendor.

What carried Cindy through? Making space for quiet prayer, persevering, and accepting help from others. In the process she realized that she was blessed with the gifts to inspire, encourage, and connect with other people. One of her clients recently said, "There is something truly special about Cindy. She is a daily inspiration!"

The truth is my sister has always been unique and matchless. But it took stepping out to grow and discover her talents. That first "yes" to follow her inner voice opened the door to many more. It was risky, but Cindy learned she was much more capable than she thought. Had she not persevered in discovering her talents and how she was meant to use them; had she not stepped out in courage, Cindy would never be where she is today — and would not have blessed all those she has met and helped since.

What about you? Where do you feel called? What's in the way? No matter your age or abilities, your stresses or challenges, God invites you to have the courage to use your talents in order to grow in your splendor.

Today, begin to explore these questions. Keep sitting with them, praying about them, talking with others. Write down what you discover.

Oftentimes, my Lord, fear and doubt stand in my way.
Remove the obstacles that block me
from doing all You call me to.
Please make it clear what I am to do.
I ask for the grace of courage, perseverance, and hope.
Please let me trust you to fill in what's needed
for me to go for it.
I love You, Lord.
You are my Savior,
the Divine Architect
of my soul.
Help me to go forward,
with You leading me.
Amen.

"*God knows*
WHAT HE IS DOING,
as for me, I have no idea. Nor do I know
what He will make out of me. But what I do
know is that His work is the best possible and
it is perfect."

– Self-Abandonment to Divine Providence
by Fr. Jean Pierre de Caussad

Reflection ⑩
....

The Surprise of Surrender

> *"Indeed, like clay in the hand of the potter, so are you in my hand."*
> — *Jeremiah 18:6*

A long time ago, I was in a difficult relationship with a handsome young man and found myself fearfully mouthing the words, "Lord, if he's not for me, take him out of my life…" And then quickly I added, "But replace him…don't leave me alone!" It was as if I were holding my breath, so afraid of the next step, so afraid of giving God the reins.

Surrender is sometimes like that; it's a battle to let go, and yet, in the end, the only voice worth trusting is the Lord's. His agenda is always for our good. Even though I tried to put parameters on turning that relationship over, the next stage was a period of aloneness, until a few years later when my husband, Don, entered the door of my heart and nothing has ever been the same.

I struggle with surrender — perhaps because I've always connected it with resignation and submission. But it's not about that at all; instead, it's an invitation to sink into our Savior's hands and trust Him.

Surrendering is the deep realization that you may not get what you want. No, you may not…you may get even more! But it's hard to trust this in the moment because surrender doesn't always feel good. It involves embracing mystery and dying to yourself, your fears, your ego, and the shadows and compulsions that keep you holding on. But as long as you keep clutching, your splendor won't shine.

Scripture reveals the exquisite story of how God is able to shape us when we surrender:

"Arise and go down to the potter's house; there you will hear my word." I went down to the potter's house and there he was, working at the wheel. Whenever the vessel of clay he was making turned out badly in his hand, he tried again, making another vessel of whatever sort he pleased. Then the word of the Lord came to me: "Can I not do to you, house of Israel, as this potter has done?— oracle of the Lord. Indeed, like clay in the hand of the potter, so are you in my hand, house of Israel" (Jer 18:2-6).

As we begin to surrender more of our lives to God, He is able to mold us into the women He has called us to be. If we don't allow God to remake us, we risk becoming like stale, old clay. A dear artist friend of mine explained that not only does clay become brittle and dried out without gentle massaging, but when it drops, it shatters. Yet all it takes is a gentle massaging and water to remold it again. It's the same with you and me.

No matter what has gone on in your life, your surrender allows you to be remade in the hands of the Potter. His hands provide the gentle massaging and the life-giving water that will bring you to a new life of splendor.

Living your splendor requires daily surrender. In those small daily acts of letting go, you slowly fall into the loving arms of our Savior.

Today, ask the Lord to remove any fears of surrendering, letting go or changing. Re-read Jeremiah 18:4-6, and insert your name in place of house of Israel. Then, think about an area of your life where you're holding on too tightly and ask God for the grace to let go. Hand over the reins and see where He leads you.

"Whenever the vessel of clay he was making turned out badly in his hand, he tried again, making another vessel of whatever sort he pleased. Then the word of the Lord came to me: "Can I not do to you, house of Israel, as this potter has done?—oracle of the Lord. Indeed, like clay in the hand of the potter, so are you in my hand, house of Israel" (Jer 18:4-6).

Father God, in the name of Jesus, I give You my life.
Regardless of my fears and doubts, I trust in You.
I surrender.
You know the longings of my heart, I turn them over to You,
trusting in Your miraculous power and tenderness.
Please grant me Your peace and show me where
to act and where to let go.
I long for newness and freshness in my life.
Please remake me, Jesus.
Give me the strength to surrender each and every moment.
I love You.
Amen.

"I've often

pointed my finger at others, blaming them.
I've wanted someone to 'rescue me,' give me
the answers, fix my hurt, fill the void, and
when it didn't happen, I became like a child
at times, wanting my way, demanding,
pushing and kicking – mostly internally –
until one day I finally saw it: I was afraid.

All the while I was pointing one finger at
others, there were four fingers pointing back
at me, challenging me to look at myself.

As long as I kept blaming others for my
situation, I didn't have to take action or step
out; I didn't have to face that I was afraid...
afraid that I wasn't good enough, and didn't
have what it takes."

– From my prayer journal

Reflection ⑪

Rise and Shine

"Little girl, I say to you, arise!" — Mark 5:41

*H*ave you ever been relegated to a role that didn't quite fit, that didn't seem to resonate with your true self? Have you ever felt like you were held back, dismissed, passed over, or excluded? I have. I've been pulled between fully being myself, questioning whether that was too much or too little, and doing what others expected of me.

I came to think that maybe God didn't want me to be fully myself; maybe He didn't want me to be outgoing or energetic, or to shine. Maybe these qualities weren't feminine or humble enough. Maybe He was the one holding me down.

It wasn't until a few years ago that I realized it was actually the opposite: that Jesus was my Liberator, the One who was calling me to be fully myself — to rise up! It happened in 2011, an event I referred to earlier in this book. I was speaking at a large women's conference about who we are as women – women of splendor. The truth was, as I addressed each and every woman in that audience, I was actually speaking even more to myself.

What I learned that weekend, and still am learning today, is that God isn't the one holding you or me back. He's the one lifting us up as women, bringing us to freedom and self-discovery. Not the way the culture always models it, but in a way that's life-giving and in harmony with our deepest identity.

This liberation is not about trying to be a man, or another woman we know or admire. My spiritual director has told me over and over again that some of the circumstances that I had longed for in my life as a young woman — and even in the early years of middle age — were not and continue not to be God's will for me. God calls you and me to a deeper identity — one that arises from the God of the Universe and isn't dependent upon other people or circumstances.

The good news is that God can bless us with happiness that we never thought possible, a happiness that is better than the circumstances we yearn for — and much longer lasting. I've seen this in my own life. He can liberate us, leading us to His truth about who we are. With time, we'll be able to connect the dots and see how it all brings us to wholeness.

Regardless of your experience, the Lord can call you forth and bring you to wholeness. He also wants to heal you of any beliefs you have that you're not good enough, that you're not lovable and delightful the way you are. He wants you to know that being you, the woman He made you to be, is wonderful! He invites you to rise up, to no longer be suppressed or afraid, to no longer be relegated to "the quiet one," or hide in the safety of never stepping out, or hang back, questioning if you're good enough. The Lord is your Liberator.

Looking back, I can see that whenever I tried to reconcile myself to the idea that God was holding me down or causing me to settle, I never experienced interior peace — never. On the other hand, I still remember how liberating it was to discover my own voice — and to use it. I gained an understanding that Wow, God, this is You calling me to be fully me! That experience has occurred when I've stepped out, when He's given me the grace to "arise." One way of living brings angst, depression, sadness, and despair; the other — God's way — brings consolation, freedom, and peace. If you're ever grappling with whether something you want or feel is from God, use the peace you experience — or lack thereof — as a barometer.

If your identity and self-worth are in need of healing, the Lord invites you to rise up. Ask for Our Lady's help — she uniquely understands what it is to be a woman and will walk with you, teaching you to become the woman God calls you to be.

Lord, I love You.
I repent of any jealousy, resentment, or judgment towards
those who have hurt me.
I am sorry.
Please give me Your peace.
Please fill me with a newfound sense of Your love and acceptance.
It hurts to feel alone. Please fill my emptiness. Heal my hurts. Bless those who
have hurt me inadvertently or otherwise, and bless those I may have hurt.
Please give me the grace to arise, and to be fully myself.
Help me to know what that looks like for me.
Dear Lady, walk with me this day — please help me to persevere, to shine.
May I be grateful. I love You, Lord.
I trust You.
I thank You for taking care of me.
Thank You for making me whole and complete.
I ask all of this in Your name, Lord.
Amen.

"*faith is*

about accepting mystery. Mystery isn't about
certainty, it's about trusting and moving
forward one step at a time with our Lord."

– From my prayer journal

Reflection ⑫

Living the Mystery

> *"Behold, I am the handmaid of the Lord. May it be done to me according to your word." — Luke 1:38*

If you're anything like me, you like to have a plan; you want to know what's going on and what to expect. But each of us is invited to trust the Lord with the unknown and to accept the mystery of life. It's not easy, but we have a model and companion in our Blessed Mother. By living the mystery of her own earthly life, Mary lived her splendor.

When the angel Gabriel came to Mary, he begins his message by saying, *"Hail, oh highly favored one."* But when you read the Scriptures, Mary's life certainly doesn't look like someone whose status is "highly favored." Why didn't God make life easier for His highly favored daughter?

Honestly, if I were about to give birth in a stable full of animals, I would have said, "Joseph, whoa, whoa, whoa… there's a problem here. There's no way it can be God's will for me to deliver His Son in this place — you must have taken a wrong turn! Now where's that angel when I need him, the one who had all those nice things to say to me?"

But Our Lady didn't say such things. She accepted what she didn't understand.

Soon afterwards, Mary and Joseph had to flee in the middle of the night with baby Jesus to escape Herod, who was killing all the newborn children to ensure his lineage as king. Later, when Mary went to the temple with her baby to fulfill Jewish law, Simeon tells her that *"a sword will also pierce your heart...."* Then there was the loss of the Christ-child in the temple — Mary and Joseph weren't told where to find their Son and spent days and nights searching for Him. Of course, there could have been no greater suffering in Our Lady's life than watching her beloved Son be condemned to death and nailed to a cross.

Is this really the life of a *"highly favored one"*? It doesn't seem to make a lot of sense. And yet Mary persevered, even in her greatest agony. She was the Mother of God, but she never had it easy. She was never handed a blueprint for her life. It was her humility, trust, patience, and reflective heart that gave her the stamina and courage to stay the course.

You and I are invited to live this kind of life, too. As we encounter heartaches and face circumstances that leave us wondering where God could possibly be, Mary is there for us. In the unknowns, the mystery, she helps us. Mary — our model of splendor who carried the King of Splendor within her womb — really does get it; she lived the mystery herself, and she will help you and me to do the same if we ask her. When God's will doesn't make sense in our lives, Mary reminds us to step back, take a breath, let go of control, and give thanks, trusting that God will give us the grace to believe.

Today, ask Mary to be your companion as you live out the mystery in your own life. Speak to Mary about your problems, your worries, and the things you don't understand, asking her to pray for you to have the same kind of trust, faith, and perseverance that she had. If you haven't before, now is a good time to invite Mary into your life as a mother and a friend.

Hail Mary, full of Grace,
The Lord is with thee.
Blessed art thou among women,
and blessed is the fruit of thy womb, Jesus.
Holy Mary, Mother of God,
pray for us sinners now,
and at the hour of death.
Amen.

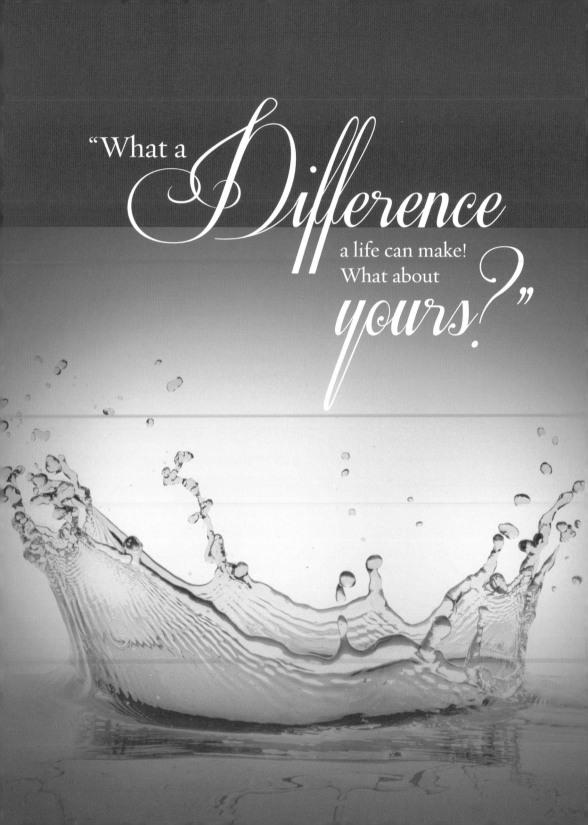

"What a *Difference* a life can make! What about *yours?*"

Reflection 🅫

Baby Cindi's Splendor

"The Little Pebble in a Big Pond"

A precious little baby
So lovely to behold
Her rosy cheeks, her dark, dark hair,
Her parents' love played such a part
She was a gift-right from the heart

Her life was short, we all agree
Yet was fulfilled, we all can see
At three days young, God took her home
He gave us just a peek

But from that precious baby girl
His work was then complete
This tiny little pebble
Used in God's Master plan
Will ripple in the Father's pond
Directed by His hand.

Live on dear precious little one
Until one day we meet
To live forever, in God's house
No longer, just a peek

~ Mary Anne Sansone, beloved grandmother

There once was a little girl whose family loved her long before she was born and anticipated her arrival with great excitement. What they didn't know was that she would be born with a respiratory condition which would take her life three days later. Although her older sister had survived the same condition — and her three younger siblings would also go on to survive it, for this little dark-haired beauty, it was not to be the same.

This baby was born and then she died. In the world's eyes, three days of life isn't nearly enough to make a difference, not enough time to "be somebody." But that couldn't be further from the truth.

As a result of this little girl's life, albeit so very brief, a treasured lifelong friendship was established between her parents and the Carmelite Sisters of the Divine Heart of Jesus, in particular a dear and holy sister named Sister Mary Rose. The sister's influence on the family, and the extended family, led to a growth in their faith and an increased love of the Church.

Under the leadership of this baby's beloved grandfather, a Catholic day care was also established for the Carmelite Sisters which helped thousands of children and their families, and as the years passed, this relationship led to something else: A facility for those in their "wisdom years."

So much fruit born from one short, little life!

A great deal happened to the family through the years. Life continued on and the memories and thoughts of their little girl warmed their hearts and continued to bring them love, a connection to Heaven, and a sense of comfort.

All of this from a little life that barely had time to breathe.

That little girl never graduated from college, never received a Master's degree or Doctorate. She never became a great lawyer, received any awards, or became a superb athlete. She never knew what it was to sing, or dance, or perform. She never experienced what it was like to date a nice boy or hold his hand, or dance in the arms of her daddy.

No, none of that, and yet she lived fully, she was pure love, the kind of love and presence that you forever hold in your heart…the kind of love that brings a family to their knees and teaches them lessons for a lifetime.

I know all of this to be true in the depths of my heart because that baby girl was my daughter — my Cindi. It's been more than 33 years ago that she died and I know — and my dear husband, her Daddy, knows — from having held that 7 lbs. 7 oz. little beauty in our arms the difference one life can make.

Cindi's little life cut through all the superficiality to the core of the human heart. In her life there was no time for pretense or facades…no time. I wonder what it would be like to live everyday like that — how freeing, how beautiful! Cindi drew out the best in everyone who was blessed to encounter her…simply by being Cindi.

What about you? Does your life bring out the best in others? You and I were created to live from our essence, our splendor. Prayer and the sacraments can help us discover that, and in turn, our lives will draw out the best in others. The way we live each day can be a stumbling block or a beacon of light for everyone around us.

Every life is designed, created, and brought to fullness by the Divine Architect of the universe. No life is worthless. There are no cast-offs, none. Your life, your splendor, is the difference the world needs right now.

Today, ask the Lord to help you reclaim your sense of how important and unique your own life is. Ask Him to reveal the steps you can take to let your splendor shine. Ask Him for the grace to cooperate with His life-giving plan for your life.

Lord, thank You that You know the days of my life.
Thank You that You have provided just
enough time for what You have planned for my life.
Please give me the freedom to become all
You created me to be.
Please God, may I be emptied of ego
and begin this moment reliving my life.
May I be Your life-giving difference in the world
and when the voice of the father of lies
brings me down I call upon the
Heavenly armies to stand guard over my mind and heart,
to remind me of my legacy.
Heal me of my internal wounds.
I love You, Jesus.
I long to make a difference with You.
I ask this in the name of Jesus.
Amen

the part You wrote for *me*

"I play so many GAMES.

I have so many faces...I run so many races that need not be run by me... Oh Lord, dear Lord, Great Author of the play. May I in wisdom learn the only part that I need play is the part You wrote for me, the part You wrote for *me.*"

– Joni Earickson Tada, Author, Singer, Founder and CEO of Joni and Friends International Disability Center

(a diving accident in 1967 left Joni Earickson, then 17, a quadriplegic)

Reflection ⓮
....
A Divided Heart

> *"Trust in [Him] with all your heart, [and] on your own intelligence do not rely; in all your ways be mindful of Him, and He will make straight your paths." — Proverbs 3:5-6*

*D*o you have a divided heart? I did and at times, still do — I have a heart that prays and trusts in God and a heart that relies on myself.

Having a divided heart is like being divided against yourself; it's a tug of war, only the tug of war is inside of you, with you pulling at one end and then tugging from the other end, fighting against yourself. In the midst of this division there is overthinking, justifying, ego, drama, and rationalizing with "feel good" moments, only to be back to the mess again. It's exhausting and diminishing.

I invite you to nip this in the bud. The moment you find yourself divided and in conflict, call on the Lord. Step back, pause, and remind yourself where peace is found, not in the tug-of-war and the justifications, but rather in uniting the division, the conflict, to Jesus on the cross. Lord, I offer this up to You for ____, trusting that You will be true to Your word and bring good out of all things. Take a moment and consider where your own sin and fear are contributing to the division in your heart and ask God for His forgiveness and love.

A divided heart is never quiet, but, a heart at rest totally belongs to Christ and is at peace, even in the midst of difficulty.

If you long for a restful heart, remember that God meets you in this desire and will bring you to wholeness. He understands. He created you; He knows you. He knows what brings you down and what makes you excited. He loves you. When you look to the Lord in trust, you are not divided. You become what you see and in Him there is no division.

No one can be happy with a divided heart. A dear friend and religious sister shared the following story with me, which is a take on an old Cherokee legend called "The Wolves Within:"

Once there was a young Native American girl who went to her wise grandmother. She told her grandmother that inside of her it seemed like there were two voices: One was jealous, competitive, fearful, worrisome, self-critical, and insecure. The other was one of encouragement, action, strength, kindness, and love, particularly towards herself… a voice that said not to settle.

The grandmother listened and said, "My daughter, you have two wolves living within you. One is filled with greed, selfishness, control, fear, and the illusion that you're not good enough. And that wolf will divide you against yourself. He'll rip you apart. And then there's the other wolf. He tells you that you're swift and strong. You're beautiful and kind. You're made for greatness." The wise grandmother went on to say, "These two wolves cannot live together. It's impossible."

The young girl then hesitantly asked, "Which one will live?"

And her grandmother smiled and answered quietly, "The one that you feed."

The one that you feed. Which voice are you feeding — division or peace?

Today, consider which heart you are nurturing by your thoughts and action. Then ask God to help you choose to follow the heart that leads to peace and love.

Lord, I love You.
I wish to be whole.
I surrender my heart to You —
my fears, my sins, and my worries.
I give them all to You. I believe.
Help my lack of belief.
Show me today Your way and when
the evil one injects fear and tempts me
to jealousy, resentment, and hopelessness,
please give me the grace
to turn my back on the father of lies.
Please Lord, let there be no division in my heart.
I desire to listen to Your voice,
to live Your ongoing will in my life.
I repent of having a divided heart.
I desire a whole heart, Your heart;
a heart of love without division.
I ask all of this in Jesus' name.
Amen

"*Dear Lord*

if this is how you treat your friends,
no wonder you have so few!"

— St. Teresa of Avila

Reflection 15

What Anger Will Teach You

> *I do not at all understand the mystery of grace — only that it meets us where we are but does not leave us where it found us.*
> —Anne Lamott, *Traveling Mercies: Some Thoughts on Faith*

Not long ago, after struggling with disappointment after disappointment, I found myself sad and tearful. I spoke to my spiritual director and without missing a beat, he asked if I was angry with God. "Well, I shouldn't be angry; I mean, lots of people have it much worse than I do, and I know God is good, but I'm really struggling with this one. I shouldn't be angry!" I told him. And then I found myself saying, "Well, God could have changed this and hasn't; I really don't know what He wants." And soon I realized I was indeed angry with God and afraid to admit it.

My spiritual director taught me a great lesson that day: That it's okay to be angry, even with God. I have to trust the Lord enough to be honest about what I feel, but I can never stop there. After expressing to Him all of my anger, resentment, and sadness, I'm also called to listen. Expressing myself is only part of the process — listening is the other.

When we listen, we learn — about ourselves, about other people, about God's own heart and His will for our lives. Because anger so often makes us feel out of control and miserable, we think of it as bad. But emotions are neither good nor bad; they're simply part of what it means to be human. Anger provides us with helpful information — it tells us that something is wrong somewhere. Instead of simply letting the emotion of anger take over, we need to bring it to the Lord and find out what it's trying to say. When we allow ourselves to be transformed by what we learn in prayer, we are living our splendor.

If we bring our anger to God and listen to Him in silence, we may begin to notice that behind it are things like: jealousy, frustration, confusion, fatigue, pride, impatience, misunderstanding, self-righteousness, and, above all, fear. And when we identify what's going on inside us, we can address the root of the anger and pray through it.

The secret to letting go of whatever is empowering our anger always lies in forgiveness — of ourselves, others, and God. Forgiveness is never easy, but the Lord gives us the grace to do it. Most of the time it's a process; it doesn't happen all at once.

Sometimes thinking of how the Lord has forgiven us helps us forgive someone else.

We should also remember that there is something called "righteous anger" — the kind of emotion we may feel in the face of injustice, exploitation, falsehood, ugliness, and evil. Righteous anger can lead us to positive action and change. This kind of anger stems from a sense of justice and hope — it doesn't make us bitter or hard-hearted.

Prayer and conversation with those we trust will help us discern our powerful emotions and learn to use them to live our splendor.

Today, take some silent time to be with the Lord and practice listening. Ask the Lord, what are You teaching me? What is it that's going on with me?

Lord God I praise You and give You glory.
Thank You for the gift of our relationship.
Thank You for Your acceptance of all of me.
Thank You for Your mercy.
Please Lord keep me from turning in on myself; rather, give me
the grace and confidence to look to You, trusting that You'll
heal and touch me and restore my soul.
I love You, Lord.
Please place Your healing hand upon my soul
(and make clear to me what's going on).
I offer my anger to You and trust in Your healing Hand.
Amen.

"Guard

my first springs of thought and will,
and with Thyself my spirit fill."

– Thomas Ken, "Awake, My Soul, and
with the Sun," Morning Hymn, 1695

Reflection ⑯

Morning Glory

"And in the morning you will see the glory of the Lord." — Exodus 16:7

*T*here is something magical, expectant, and peaceful about the early morning hours. It's a time that invites the words of Samuel in the Old Testament: *"Speak, Lord, for your servant is listening" (3:10).*

Waking up early to meet our Savior helps us to begin the day in a grace-filled place. So much clamors for our attention during the day, yet as the sun rises at dawn, in the quiet, there's a real sense of being alone with God. As the planet seems to sleep, it's a perfect time to hear the whisper of the Savior in your heart, to come in touch with Splendor Himself before the whirl of your life begins.

I remember a time when I was particularly overwhelmed and stressed and saw no way out. I did the very thing I am encouraging you to do – to meet Jesus in the morning. The comfort and solace it brought me is still vivid in my mind today. The desperation and confusion dissipated and solutions came. In those early morning moments, I began to see light in the tunnel that had seemed so dark.

The morning hours are a time to pour your heart out to Jesus, to rest in His arms, to pause, speak, ask, and listen. As you anticipate the day to come, imagine walking hand in hand with Him who gives you this day, and leads you through your tasks and commitments. In the freshness of the morning, the day is like an open stage and you are awaiting the lights. One day, that curtain will rise for the last time — how sad it will be if we've missed out on starting each day with our Lord, if only for a few minutes.

Not long ago, while I was sitting in church, a fun loving, straight-talking woman — I'll call her "Bonnie" — came in struggling with her two oxygen tanks. As she plopped down before the Blessed Sacrament, breathing heavily, she said aloud, "Hi God, I made it. …Thank You." After Mass she remarked, "Every day is a gift."

About two weeks later, I noticed Bonnie wasn't there. I asked about her and learned that although she had a set-back, Bonnie was eager to rejoin her church community. I breathed a sigh of relief and smiled as I thought of her keeping time for the retired priest so his homily would be brief and to the point. She would always remind him to pray our habitual Hail Mary for the unborn. Bonnie was a wonderful lady, feisty and full of life.

Then one day, I learned she had died. During his homily that morning, Father mentioned he had to keep it short as he was being watched and timed. Bonnie is still missed by many, even by someone she never knew personally — me.

There will come a day when, like Bonnie, the light of the morning will lead each of us elsewhere. None of us knows how many more days we have on this earth, how many more mornings we can greet the Lord and begin our day in His embrace.

Evening can be a special time, but it doesn't bring the freshness and hope that morning does. It wasn't easy for my friend Bonnie to get to church to spend time with God, but she made it happen. Day after day she began each morning by meeting her Savior. I can't help but wonder if when Bonnie met with the Lord the day she went home He said, "Hi Bonnie. You made it…. Thank you!"

If you're like me and wake up diving into the day, or, if you want to pull the sheets up over your head and not move, consider choosing one morning this week where you will rise and go off to a quiet space to meet the Lord. Light a candle, bring a crucifix, a Bible, a rosary — whatever helps you to meet the Lord.

Some years ago my son, Craig, shared with me a simple practice for meeting Jesus that he had learned from a wise priest. Father advised him to pull up a chair, imagine Jesus sitting there, and then to take a seat across from Him and start talking about his day or whatever was on his mind and heart. Father suggested doing this for about five to 15 minutes and said that if Craig found himself continually complaining, to stop for a moment, think of what was good, and thank the Lord for it.

I can tell you that this little practice has been a blessing to me, particularly on those days that look to be overwhelming. So I encourage you, as your day begins, to "pull up a chair" and have a conversation with the Architect of your soul. Imagine Him sitting there, leaning toward you. He's in no rush — you're His purpose for being there. Start your day with the Lord and remember that He will accompany you throughout the day.

*Lord, thank You for the opportunity to meet with
You in the beginning hours of the day.
Please give me the grace and discipline to rise to greet You,
to experience a new beginning each and
every morning of my life; to purposefully
seek silence so as to greet You.
I love You.
Amen*

"*We know that*

all things work for good for those who
love God, who are called according to
His purpose."

— Romans 8:28

Reflection ❶⑦

....

Being Thankful When Life Is Hard

> *"He bends down to me and hears my cry... and puts a new song into my mouth." — Psalm 40:1-3*

The year was 1983. I had given birth to two beautiful little girls — first our daughter, Annie, and then, one year later, Cindi. It was picture perfect, and yet, as I shared previously, this bliss was not to last. Our beloved Cindi was called home to heaven only a few days after her birth. Even now, my heart constricts and tears well up in my eyes at the thought of my precious baby daughter.

A short time after Cindi's passing, a dear and holy man shared with me the power of praise. He told me that through the many losses he experienced in life, he found hope and healing when he praised and thanked God for everything, even the losses and the hurt; trusting that God would bring good out of it all. He encouraged me to praise God for my loss.

I was a little baffled. How do you praise and thank God for deep pain and loss?

I remember thinking that I'd be a phony; that there was no way I could do that. How could I possibly thank God for allowing my baby girl to die? And yet, I longed to be one with God, to experience His peace, and to have relief from my pain. In my desperation, in my deep desire for healing and wholeness, I found myself mouthing the words, I praise You and thank You,

Lord, for taking my baby girl to Heaven. I praise You and thank You in this tremendous loss. As I spoke those words my heart cried out, Please Lord help me, Your will be done, I believe, help my lack of belief. Let me play the part that You wrote for me. Looking back, it was almost as if from that moment on a change took place. In time, my heart and my soul began to conform to that prayer, and slowly, by God's grace, the healing came. Heaven now feels that much closer.

We read in Matthew's Gospel: *"Learn from the way the wild flowers grow. They do not work or spin....If God clothes the grass of the field, which grows today and is thrown into the oven tomorrow, will He not much more provide for you?"(6:28-30)* And yet sometimes in life there seems to be a disconnect between the Word of God and reality. The whole idea of our Heavenly Father watching out for us, caring for us, was difficult to accept when my arms were empty and my baby's crib was bare. And yet the promise of God's word is always unfolding and ever true.

I know you have experienced heartache. Sometimes it's tempting to hold onto the hurts and losses like coveted trophies. At some level, we don't want to let them go, and it's important that we never ignore the pain of loss, of telling God how we hurt. But we must also allow newness to come into our lives. Consider praising God for your hurts and your sufferings. He is faithful to His promises. Praying, being honest with God, partaking in the sacraments, letting others into our pain and sadness, and allowing time to pass are all part of the road to wholeness and peace.

Today, especially if you are burdened and in pain, praise God in your suffering. He, too, knows suffering. Remember, Jesus modeled thanksgiving and a deep acceptance in the midst of His approaching Passion, even after His betrayal. Thank Him for the good He will bring from your sadness, and for His promises. Ask Him to help you surrender any hurts you have been holding on to. Ask Him to strengthen and heal you.

My Lord and my God, please strengthen and heal me.
You know the longings and desires of my heart —
You encourage me to share them with
You and yet I continue to remain
broken and downhearted.
Oh my God, please give me a new song.
Heal me.
May my heart once again feel joy.
May my life take up a new song.
Without You all is impossible.
You are my Hope, my Shield, my Protector.
I trust in You, my Lord.
I praise You and give You glory in this, my sadness and loss.
I trust that Your mercy and desire for
my good is greater than my longing.
My God, please heal my tattered Heart.
I accept Your holy will in my life.
Oh God have mercy.
Amen.

"WELCOME *to this* $\mathcal{M}$*agical place.*"—Eva

Reflection ⓲

....

Eva's Splendor

> *"Friendships begun in this world will be taken up again, never to be broken off."* — *St. Francis de Sales*

A few years ago, I was blessed to encounter a lovely woman — I will call her "Eva." One of Eva's eyes was permanently closed, the other was disfigured, and she limped with a slow gait. I learned later that her physical challenges were due to an accident when she was 21. While Eva would never be found on the cover of a fashion magazine, her inner beauty and splendor shone.

I saw Eva for the first time at a posh health club as she came around the corner to the front desk. She spoke to the attractive young woman behind the counter who took little notice of her, but Eva seemed unfazed. After graciously thanking the woman, Eva slowly moved forward, looked up, smiled, and remarked to no one in particular, "Oh, the balloons. Aren't they beautiful?"

I followed Eva's gaze and saw them, too, behind the reception desk. I had passed the desk more than once that day, but never noticed the balloons, even though I'm in good health with no sight problems. Eva, on the other hand, with only partial sight, could see something most people missed.

Eva and I ended up in conversation, and she was genuine and delightful. She asked how long I had been coming to the health club and when I explained that I was new, she said, "Welcome to this magical place." I told her I was

79

surprised I hadn't noticed the balloons before, and that I was grateful she had pointed them out since without her, I wouldn't have noticed them at all. She hesitated with her response, as if she was unsure whether to share her next thought, but she did. "Slowing down really is a blessing, "she said, "because I'm slow, I notice."

Eva radiated her splendor. She "showed up" for life; she didn't just go through the motions. It couldn't have been easy for her. She could have made some very different decisions; she could have given up, becoming bitter and living small, safe, and hidden. But she didn't. And in the process, she gave a total stranger like me a treasured gift.

And now, years later, I remember the lovely lady named Eva who helped me see the "beautiful balloons" that I had been missing. It was one of those moments in life that you don't forget. Eva taught me the importance of slowing down and noticing the beauty that's around me every day.

Do you miss the colorful balloons in your life? Do you slow down enough to notice all the little things God provides each day to help lift your mind and heart? When we do slow down, the world really does seem more magical.

Today, ask the Lord to help you grow in your awareness of the beauty around you — in the small things, in the people and surroundings you encounter each day. God is in all of it and speaks to you there.

Lord Jesus, so often I see the "ugly," the "troubling,"
the "burdensome" and miss out on the
"balloons" of life, the rainbows, the "new."
Oh Lord, please give me the grace of seeing with Your eyes.
Please open my eyes to see beyond the ups and downs of my life,
my moods, my troubles, my sadness.
Please give me the grace to emotionally and
physically quiet down, to be light-hearted and present
to the many joyful, spontaneous surprises in life.
I love You.
Mercifully hear my prayer.
Amen.

"Remember, oh most

gracious Virgin Mary, that never was it known that anyone who fled to thy protection, implored thy help, or sought thy intercession was left unaided. Inspired by this confidence, I fly unto thee, oh virgin of virgins, my Mother; to thee do I come, before thee I stand, sinful and sorrowful. Oh mother of the Word Incarnate, despise not my petitions, but in thy mercy hear and answer me. Amen."

– Memorare prayer

Reflection 19

....

The Power of the Rosary

> *"There is no problem, I tell you, no matter how difficult it is, that we cannot resolve by the prayer of the Holy Rosary."*
> — Sr. Lucia dos Santos (Fatima visionary)

Years ago when I was a young mother, our dear friend Sr. Mary Rose encouraged my husband and me to pray the rosary as a family. She invited us to "step into the protection of the rosary." She said that when you take that step, Our Lady enfolds you, your family, and your loved ones into her mantle of love and peace.

Through the years, Don and I have reflected on those early days of praying the rosary with our kids. We were certainly no model family: before the Sacred Heart altar in our home, the kids would fidget, get distracted, want to be held, and sometimes misbehave. Don and I would often snap impatiently, grab for one, separate others, and at times practically fall asleep. Sometimes I'd be angrier when it ended than before we had begun! But we continued, thanks to the grace of Our Lord (and the encouragement and support of Sr. Mary Rose).

God doesn't ask for perfect prayer. He asks for a desire and a first step. The rosary is a very powerful prayer if you want to see change in your life. For some, the rosary can be a little daunting, but it's a profound way to share in the Lord's life and to let Him change your heart. You can give no greater gift to your family.

If you begin with one decade, and do it day after day, you'll soon see miracles in your life, and the lives of your loved ones. History is full of such stories. Over and over, Christ grants miracles on a grand scale, against all odds, for those who are humble enough to pick up this spiritual treasure and meditate on its mysteries.

God reads our hearts and knows the purity of our intentions. I'm so grateful that we didn't have to be a perfect family to pray the rosary together. I'm also grateful for my parents who modeled the rosary, and for Sr. Mary Rose, a light in my life. Don and I believe if ever there was one thing we did right in raising our children, it was to pray the rosary together. I have seen its powerful fruits over the years.

I encourage you to "take up your rosary" when you're happy, sad, encouraged, discouraged, angry, peaceful — any time at all. It is the Lord's gift to us in our journey of life. The Savior of the world gives us His Mother and the light of the rosary to dispel the darkness of the evil one, and accompanies us along the journey. What a joy to be in her company!

Pope Saint Pius X said "[t]he Rosary is the most beautiful and the most rich in graces of all prayers: it is the prayer that touches most the Heart of the Mother of God... and if you wish peace to reign in your homes, recite the family Rosary."

Today, take that first step and pray one Our Father, ten Hail Mary's, and one Glory Be. Mary will help you.

Oh God —
Whose only begotten Son, by His life, death, and resurrection,
has purchased for us the rewards of eternal salvation —
grant, we beseech Thee, that while
meditating on these mysteries
of the most holy Rosary of the Blessed Virgin Mary,
that we may both imitate what they contain
and obtain what they promise,
through Christ our Lord. Amen.

Most Sacred Heart of Jesus, have mercy on us.

Immaculate Heart of Mary, pray for us.

Eve grasped in distrust but *Mary* received in faith.

Reflection 20

Letting Go

> "There are many things in my life to which I cling as with a clinched fist
> — my possessions for sure but the immaterial things as well —
> the work I do, the position I hold, the friends I have, my ideas, my
> principles, my image. If I should open my fist, they still remain.
> Nothing drops out. But my hands are open.... After a while, if I am
> willing to remain long enough with open hands, the Lord will come..."
> — Peter G. van Breemen, S.J.

One day in prayer I came across the Scripture passage of Jesus ridding a person of an evil spirit. I remember thinking Lord, what do I need to be rid of? The answer that came surprised me: Possessiveness.

What does it mean to be possessive? With prayer, I came to see that it's what happens when we hold on, when we try to dominate the object of our love or desire. Being possessive is a lonely place of fear and grasping, and stems from insecurity — that sense of not feeling loved enough. The truth is, you and I are completely and totally loved by God. We know that, we hear that, but do we believe it? The mere fact that you exist is proof of God's love. It's as if Jesus says to you and me, *I choose you. You have great significance. You are beloved to me. I reside within you.* There is security in knowing that you and I are loved like this — it brings us freedom.

The only way to live in true freedom is to truly let go. But that can be frightening. I remember praying, Lord, if I let go, what will fill the void? And once again the answer surprised me — peace. Peace is what God wants to give us to replace our possessiveness.

Many of us go through life as if our hands are clenched, holding on, grasping. This idea of clenched hands struck me at one point and I realized that the only path to true happiness — to freedom — is to literally open up my hands. It's symbolic of opening up our hearts, our souls, our minds to all that God wants to give us. Now, if I find my hands clenched or my spirit grasping, I will purposely, slowly, open up my hands. This small gesture helps me to let go.

As women, we struggle particularly with possessiveness. After all, we love deeply. But true love begins with loving ourselves…confident and mindful of our self-worth. True love is respectful of another's freedom and is charitable and self-sacrificing. Those of us with children may find ourselves wanting to be the recipient of all of their affections and love. This tendency may show up in many other relationships — with family members, spouses, significant others, friends, co-workers.

I know a handsome young man who's dated quite a bit and remember meeting one of the young women he was seeing. I was taken aback by how possessive she was of him. She appeared to have no sense of her splendor, and seemed so afraid of losing him. She was lovely but didn't realize it, and I wanted to say to her, "Honey, do you realize what you possess? Do you realize you are a treasure and have the power to do so much good? This guy may or may not be the right one for you and demanding or wanting him to be will not make it so. Your whole reason for being is not this man. There's a whole world waiting for you; God has a plan just for you, a plan for your joy and prosperity."

If our identity and purpose are rooted in God, we don't cling or rely solely on others for our sense of self-worth.

I've seen possessiveness in families, too, where the members seem to be vying for position. There's no sense of sharing and kindness, no collaborative spirit

– instead, attention-grabbing, resentment, and jealousy surface if another appears to receive more. The irony is that when we grasp and try to hold on to happiness, we find ourselves empty and in conflict.

Behind our possessiveness is often brokenness, hurt, and a lack of healing. These often cause us to act in ways that undermine our splendor. Many of us don't realize, for example, the ways we can be passive-aggressive, such as avoiding direct and clear confrontation, bottling up our feelings, sulking or pouting. If and when you feel a desire to manipulate or be unkind, or you feel jealous, immediately go to our Lord, tell Him you're sorry, and ask for His help. The more we trust in God, the more we can let people go, and surrender the need to control them.

When we really believe that in God there is more than enough love to go around, we can relax and be at peace, no longer afraid. His abundance fills all scarcity.

Lord, have mercy on me.
Please remind me that You are a God of abundance,
not scarcity.
Please heal me of the idea that there is
a limited amount of Your gifts to go around
and that I must grab what is mine and
hold on tight to prevent someone from stealing it.
Lord Jesus, heal my hurts, my insecurities,
fill me with Your love.
I long to be at peace.
I love You, Lord.
Amen

"Being in a hurry.

Getting to the next thing without fully entering the thing in front of me. I cannot think of a single advantage I've ever gained from being in a hurry. But a thousand broken and missed things, tens of thousands, lie in the wake of all the rushing...through all that haste I thought I was making up time. It turns out I was throwing it away."

— Anne Voskamp, One Thousand Gifts:
   A Dare to Live Fully Right Where You are

Reflection ㉑

The Importance of Slowing Down

> *"As I go forward with you, Lord, please strengthen the quiet voice of my conscience, your own voice, in my life. Look at me as you looked at Peter. Let your gaze penetrate my heart and indicate the direction my life must take.... Grant me, ever anew, the grace of conversion."*
> — *Adapted from Cardinal Joseph Ratzinger's Way of the Cross, 2005, shared by the Carmelite Sisters of the Most Sacred Heart of Los Angeles*

When I was in my early 40s, I was invited to join a group of faith-filled women, most of them older than I, to discuss stocks and investments. One day I showed up at our monthly meeting particularly stressed, feeling pulled in many directions. Dropping all business at hand, these wise women began speaking to me about living from the soul and encouraged me to stop living from one frenzied moment to the next; in short, to "slow down." I still remember one lovely lady who looked at me knowingly and said, "It's about the important over the urgent, not the other way around."

I began to learn what that meant. The important had to do with activities that helped me achieve my deepest, most important goals. My desire to pray a family rosary with my husband and children, develop particular relationships, and find a job in line with my heart were such examples. The urgent, on the other hand, had to do with activities that demanded my attention immediately and were usually associated with meeting the goals of someone else — like checking emails several times a day, taking work home to complete night after night, or trying to accomplish an endless list of tasks.

In the midst of all the rushing, having too much to do in too little time, and the overwhelming feeling of "it's all on me," I had forgotten what really matters, what was most important. I had lost touch with the essence and true meaning of my life. I had lost touch with the peace that only God can give. I wasn't living in compatibility with my soul.

There are always periods of busyness in our lives, but we have to be mindful of the important. We don't want to lose God and our sense of peace in the midst of it.

Living our splendor isn't about taking on more and more — in fact, it may be about taking on less — about simplifying, being more intentional, looking down the road, anticipating what it is you long for and going for it. It may be about pulling back, rediscovering the voice of Jesus within yourself, getting back to the basics, and living in the present. The still, small voice within invites you to slow down in order to think and reflect on the life to which God calls you. This helps you and me to live with purpose and to let our splendor truly shine.

How can we learn to discern God's agenda for us and distinguish it from the multiple demands and tugs on our time? My spiritual director pointed out to me one day that God's agenda never makes a slave of you. Your ego, on the other hand, can suck the freedom right out of your life. Ego is sometimes disguised as the need to please, ingratiate, and respond to everyone else's demands, which can make you a slave. Sometimes, it's the desire not to "miss out" which prompts us to attend yet another event that leaves us exhausted and resentful. Even your altruistic efforts of helping and serving others can end up making you a slave if they're not rooted in freedom and healthy boundaries.

So what do we do in the midst of all this? The answer is prayer. Prayer helps us to separate God's agenda from our own ego. The Lord will show us the way if we take some time with Him each day. Seeking His direction for your everyday life will free you to live your splendor, free you for the important.

Be careful not to fall into the trap that you don't have time for prayer. A wise friend of mine, a French religious sister, Sr. Emmanuel, said, "If you pray, you have more time. Look at Saint Teresa of Calcutta,…she daily prayed two hours before the Blessed Sacrament and in addition went to Holy Mass and prayed the rosary, and look at what she did in her life — prayer gives you more time!"

It's true: prayer helps you to slow down, experience time differently, and identify what's most important in your life. Pausing periodically throughout the day to settle ourselves, stepping away from the frenzy, consciously breathing in and out silently praying the name of Jesus can help us. Remember that Jesus Himself was constantly pulled in many directions. He lived in the tension. Scripture tells us that He had to go off in the night to be alone to pray. So He gets it; He'll lead us through the many demands in our lives to what really matters.

Oh Lord, please help me to slow down enough to see
Your hand in my life. Please bless me with peace.
It's so easy for me to get caught up in the urgency of this and that
and the many demands of my life.
May I wait on You. May I meet You daily.
May I have the courage and grace to slow it down,
to begin my day with You, to prioritize what's most important.
Please show me a way where I see no way.
Give me balance my Lord; take care of the many urgent demands on my life.
I rely and trust in You. Please help me to discern
the important over the urgent in my life.
Please help me to realize that I'm much more than what I do
and that time with You is my power.
I love you, Lord.
I ask all of this in Your name.
Amen.

Praying

"If you've been

for a while without receiving your desire, don't cease praying, for it is in persevering that you will attain your desires — continue to pray. Your prayer paves the road that leads to your desire."

— From my prayer journal

"By your perseverance you will secure your lives."

— Luke 21:19

Reflection ㉒

. . . .

When Prayers Go Unanswered

> *"Three times I begged the Lord about this, that it might leave me, but He said to me, 'My grace is sufficient for you, my power is made perfect in weakness.'"* — *2 Corinthians 12:8-9*

I know of a deeply devout couple who, after giving birth to their first born child, prayed and prayed for another child for years but never gave birth again. Another dear friend, longing for a child, suffered miscarriage after miscarriage. A devoted, faith-filled mother I know has prayed unceasingly about a split in her family and it still continues.

The Lord tells us in Scripture that whatever we ask in His name will be granted, yet often we are not gifted with what we pray for. We seek answers and ask for help, but our prayers often go unanswered and there's a temptation to give up. We wonder, what's the use?

It can be difficult to remain hopeful in the midst of seemingly unanswered prayers. But to lose heart is to give up on Him who knew the agony of the cross so much that He cried out, *"My God, my God, why have you forsaken me?"*

When I'm discouraged by unanswered prayer, I'm drawn back to my Lord through this passage in the Gospel of John: *"Do you also want to leave? Simon Peter answered Him, 'Master, to whom shall we go? You have the words of everlasting life.'"*

My spiritual director remarked to me recently: "Jesus gives us the confidence to know that God will answer, yet sometimes the answer is deeper than our understanding at the time... and the answer remains a mystery."

When our prayers aren't fulfilled, we have a decision to make: to give up on prayer or to stand in prayerful trust and perseverance believing God will bring victory out of our waiting and suffering.

Can we take God at His word, that He will bring good out of all things? We must trust in His promise.

Prayers that seem unanswered call us to continue on in faith and move forward in hope. They help us to grow in perseverance and patience, and to go deeper into the mystery of God.

Do you have a longing or need that has yet to be fulfilled or a vision yet to be realized? Take heart that the Lord hears your prayer and remains at your side. His timing is mysterious and His ways are not our ways, but we know that He is always with us, working for our good. He wants our happiness even more than we want it. I try to remember this when I find myself in that place.

Once, when I was completely disheartened after having prayed and prayed for something, I stumbled upon this Scripture passage:

I will stand at my guard post, and station myself upon the rampart; I will keep watch to see what He will say to me, and what answer He will give to my complaint. Then the Lord answered me and said: "Write down the vision; make it plain upon tablets, so that the one who reads it may run. For the vision is a witness for the appointed time, a testimony to the end; it will not disappoint. If it delays, wait for it, it will surely come, it will not be late" (Habakkuk 2:1-3).

I was particularly encouraged by the words *"it will not disappoint. If it delays, wait for it, it will surely come, it will not be late."*

God spoke to me through this passage. It was as if He were saying, *Be patient, trust, persevere… have hope. My vision is from a much wider horizon than you are able to see.*

Unanswered prayers are an indication that God is working at a deeper level in our lives. He will lead us out of our situation. It's very important to do as my spiritual director advises: "Seek the God of consolation, not the consolation of God." In other words, seek out God for who He is, not the answers you seek. Imagine a mother who is only valued by her family for her service — doing laundry, preparing meals, making beds — and her family never sits with her, experiences her love, enjoys her. Imagine how sad that would be, imagine how empty. Not just for the mother, but also for her children; think of what they would miss out on — the essence of their mom.

Today, take some time to be with Jesus. Speak of your longings, but even more, just be with Him. Tell Him you love Him; praise Him. Don't miss out on His essence. If you have unanswered prayers, look back and see what Jesus has done in other areas of your life and be consoled. Our God is a God who counts your every tear and never leaves your side. He's the God who calls you to ask for the desires of your heart. Eventually, they will be satisfied.

> *Lord Jesus,*
> *"I have called upon your name, oh Lord,*
> *from the bottom of the pit; You heard my call.*
> *Do not let your ear be deaf to my cry for help!*
> *You drew near on the day I called you:*
> *You said, 'Do not fear.' You pleaded my case,*
> *Lord, you redeemed my life."*
> *—Lamentations 3:55-58*

"*Service*
is offering assistance to someone else while
discovering YOURSELF in the process."

— From my prayer journal

Reflection ㉓

The Joy of Service

> "As each one has received a gift, use it to serve one another as good stewards of God's varied grace....Whoever serves, let it be with the strength that God supplies, so that in all things God may be glorified through Jesus Christ."
> — 1 Peter 4:10-11

When I was a young, single woman, I had illusions of finding exciting work on the East Coast and wowing folks with my amazing presence and talents. It didn't take long to discover that no one was waiting in line to snatch me up and give me the career of my dreams. No one. Instead, I ended up in a dead-end job, feeling disillusioned and unhappy.

At that time my dad was expanding his company and one evening he asked if I'd like to work with seniors in federally-subsidized housing. The offer was a far cry from what I had planned for myself, but my sad state of affairs prompted me to say yes. That decision was the beginning of a life-changing discovery: There is great joy in service.

What does service mean, exactly? Essentially, it's offering assistance to someone else while discovering yourself in the process. That's what happened to me during those years with the senior housing programs. I found a happiness and fulfillment I never expected. I spent my days not in the chaotic bright-lighted hustle of 5th Avenue where I thought I belonged, but rather, in a construction trailer in a low-income neighborhood with people in their twilight years.

While this was far from the glamorous position I had first imagined, happiness and fulfillment became my newfound friends. When I awoke each morning, I had joy and a sense of purpose. Serving others made me feel alive, vibrant, fed, purposeful, and intentional. In other words, service helped me to discover and live my splendor.

I'm not the only one who's discovered this secret. In fact, God has wired each of us for service — and for the joy and fulfillment that comes with it. Service is about extending the great love God has for you towards others.

The call to serve can come out of nowhere — like the job opportunity from my dad. But often, it needs to be intentionally sought out. There are so many ways to serve — in our families, churches, cities, communities. And there is no end to the kinds of things we can do. It's tempting to get confused about what we should take on, but the evil one likes to use that tactic to hold us back. Don't fall into that trap — just start somewhere.

No matter your age, your condition in life, your busy schedule, your seeming lack of talent or great genius, you are called to service and that service will light the way to discovering and living your splendor more deeply. Sometimes we just need the reminder; a reminder of what brings happiness. If once in a while you find yourself a little heavyhearted, reach out in service. And then, see what happens…it's amazing.

Today, ask yourself: How can I serve? Where can I make a difference? Then be quiet and listen. Spend the next week asking these questions and keep your eyes open for ways you are being invited to service. It may be a small gesture: a smile, a nod of encouragement, a note to a loved one, visiting someone, baking goodies for a neighbor. Or it may be more involved: a job change, a move, initiating and/or leading an outreach program, a mission trip, participating in hospital ministry or the pro-life movement. The Lord will show you the way He has called you to serve.

Allow me to share part of a meditation from the Magnificat that reveals to us what it is to reach out to another:

… the hand I hold is small for her age and contorted. Her limbs are terribly thin, twisted, and abnormally short, and have to be strapped in a special wheelchair. She doesn't eat the way you and I do. She is fed through a tube attached straight through her abdomen. Some would call her a vegetable. I wouldn't. Because her name is Tracy. And there's one thing she does well, despite all these, Tracy smiles. And her smile takes your breath away. You see, she is able to smile when she likes something. It's the only way she communicates. So I playfully rub the back of her neck, and whisper to her ear, Tracy, do you like this? Smile if you do… She does, and it's so sweet, you'd fall in love with her right there. I wipe her saliva with her bib, which is now soaking wet, and continue to hold her hand for the rest of the day. I go home with tears in my eyes.

…No articles written…no songs composed, no meetings held, no books read, no plans designed… All I did was hold her hand. And allowed myself to be loved by a smile. But the peace I felt! — Bo Sanchez (Magnificat, September 2015, vol. 17)

Lord God, show me the way.
Lead me to all You are calling me to become.
I long for fulfillment, for peace, for joy.
Show me how you want me to use my talents
and my presence to serve others.
Open my eyes to see Your call…
Open my ears to hear Your call.
Lord God, give me the grace to take the first step.
Don't let me hide.
I love You, Jesus.
Amen.

"*You formed* my inmost being; you knit me in my mother's womb. I praise You because I am wonderfully made; wonderful are your works! My very self You *know.*"

— Psalms 139:13-14

Reflection ㉔

"Woman on the Road"

She walks her way, alone, carrying with her, the thoughts of home.
She cannot thrive without them.
And yet, her way must be her own.
The trees of life, about her stand.
She feeds from all their fruit.
She walks her way, her eyes on God.
The Giver of her roots.
The trees must be, they are her growth.
And yet her time apart,
To walk with God,
His word to hear to satisfy her heart.

The year my mom wrote "Woman on the Road" – 1986 — I was 31 and my youngest sibling was 8; a 23 year difference between us. In those days, my mom was pulled in many directions as she fulfilled her roles as wife, mother, grandmother, daughter, sister, friend. But in the midst of it all was Mary Anne — a woman with needs and dreams of her own.

I watched my mother, in her early 50s — with four of her children grown, four still at home, and13 grandchildren — meet a new desire in her heart. She enrolled in college and graduated summa cum laude. It was a great accomplishment, and an inspiring example of living yet another facet of her splendor.

Our vocational roles as wives, mothers, daughters, sisters, professionals, friends, etc. are certainly the means by which God calls us to love and to serve, but we are more than these. On the deepest level, your vocation is to be the unique, individual person that God has made you to be — an individual woman with a splendor unlike anyone else's. I am not just my husband's wife, my children's mom, my parents' daughter, my sibling's sister, my friend's friend; I am Deby, God's one and only. And that is true of you, too.

In addition to the dreams each of us holds, there is boundless splendor within us. Life provides opportunities that invite us to show up in a different way, a new way — beyond our everyday roles, as well as in the midst of them. Sometimes it's these very situations that help you discover who you are and allow your splendor to shine and grow brighter.

When I think about this, once again my mother comes to mind. I'll never forget watching her minister to two women as they were dying — one was my dear Grandma Rosie (my mother's mother-in-law), and the other was my mother's beloved aunt. Mom was pure heart, total love. It was a remarkable thing to witness. This vivacious, attractive, active woman whom I had known as a partner to my dad, chef, hostess, leader, and disciplinarian, was completely present to these loved ones as they crossed over from this life to the next. There's a nakedness in the dying process, where all masks are removed — it's not always pretty, and not always quick — and yet, there is a sacredness, a beauty all its own. I saw my mom step into that reality. She prayed with these women, reminded them of past memories, reflected on the people who had gone ahead and were waiting for them, reassured them it was okay to move on, and nurtured them every step of the way. In those moments, I saw another dimension of my mom that I'd never seen before; she was true splendor to me.

Letting our unique selves come forth looks a lot like that. When you pay attention to what draws your heart, to what comes second nature and gives you deep meaning, when you pay attention to the voice within and are present to the needs of others, you discover more of yourself. Then you can bring that into the rest of your life, being even more of who you are in the roles that you fulfill.

Do you realize that you are more than any of your duties or roles? Yes, you are a wife, sister, daughter, mom, cook, gardener, chauffeur, professional, employer, employee, neighbor — but you are also more than all of that. You are you…with your own matchless spirit and capacity for love, with desires and capabilities that are yours alone.

Today, once again, begin to pay attention to what draws your heart. Ask God what He may be inviting you to step into and look for the opportunities that life brings to your doorstep. Have the courage to respond. Speak to the Lord from your heart and be prepared to listen.

Lord Jesus, I praise You and give You glory.
Help me to discover myself. In the midst of my roles, my jobs,
my obligations, carry me.
Help me to look on my life with
a newfound freshness and energy.
I trust in You.
Only You can show me the way.
Open my eyes…let me see past my fatigue,
my routine, my disappointments, my hurts,
my inadequacies, my confusion, my regrets.
Show me the next step you call me to.
I long to become all You created me to be.
Please give me the grace and
courage to step into my splendor.
You are the God of the universe,
You can do all things.
Do Your work in me.
I ask this in Jesus' name.
Amen.

"When I come to

a human heart in Holy
Communion, my hands are
full of all kinds of graces which I want
to give to the soul, but souls do not
even pay attention to Me. They leave
me to myself and busy themselves
with other things...they treat me as a
dead object."

- St. Faustina (from her diary)

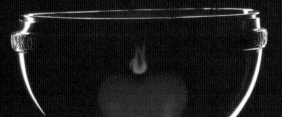

Reflection ㉕

The Bread We Can't Live Without

"I am the living bread that came down from heaven; whoever eats this bread will live forever and the bread that I will give is my flesh for the life of the world." —John 6:51

More than twelve centuries ago, around the year 750 A.D., in the Abruzzo Village of Lanciano, Italy, there lived a Basilian monk who began to doubt that the host he consecrated for Mass was the real body and blood of Christ. One day, while celebrating Mass, struggling with the idea of transubstantiation in his heart, the monk consecrated the bread and wine. After pronouncing "This is My Body…This is my Blood," something extraordinary and miraculous happened: He noticed blood dripping from the Host. It is said that after a long period of euphoric silence, with tears falling down his face, he turned to the congregation saying, "Here is the real body and blood of our Lord Jesus Christ, which He has made visible to me, that I may no longer be a disbeliever, but a believer."

The Eucharistic miracle of Lanciano is still there after all these years for pilgrims to see, and many years ago, I saw it with my very own eyes. That host I saw was indeed real human flesh and blood, and scientific studies have verified it. There's more, too: Scientists that examined the host concluded that the flesh consists of the muscular tissue of a human heart.

As I stood there in Lanciano, it really hit me…this is Jesus! How often had I forgotten that on my way up to Communion during Mass? How often had I thought of my next task, what to make for dinner, an office meeting, an issue with one of my children or my husband, what to wear for an evening out — preoccupied as I casually waltzed up the aisle and back to my pew? How often had I been distracted from the greatest reality of all time?

The Eucharistic miracle at Lanciano is further evidence that the Eucharist is indeed the Body and Blood of Jesus, veiled under the guise of bread, but nonetheless, Him. This Communion in which I so often absentmindedly participate in is truly alive!

We need to ask God for the grace to see, to recognize Him in the Eucharist. Remember the apostles on the road to Emmaus? They didn't recognize Jesus, and yet, He was with them. It was only after the breaking of the bread, that their eyes were opened and they recognized Him.

At times, maybe you and I are like the apostles on the road to Emmaus — caught up, worried, wearied, distracted, preoccupied, looking forward or behind us, missing the moment of now – of Jesus' presence to us in the moment.

The Body and Blood of Jesus heals, consoles, strengthens, and empowers us. It is food for the soul, and for our entire being.

Today, be aware of God's great love for you and His yearning to be one with you in the Holy Eucharist. Ask the Lord for greater faith in His Real Presence, and meditate on how intimate Jesus wants to be with you through the gift of His Body and Blood.

Lord God please grant that I may see...
truly see You in the Eucharist; truly believe in Your Real Presence.
I'm like Your disciples (followers) on the road to Emmaus.
You draw near to me, walk with me,
and still I do not see You...
Recognize You.
Lord I believe.
Help my unbelief.
Heal my doubt. Strengthen my faith.
Open my eyes.
I love You, Jesus, Thank You for making
Yourself available to me for always.
You are my lifeline.
Please, in Your name draw me to You. Lord,
You have the words of everlasting life.
I believe; help my unbelief!
Amen.

"Be who You are and be that well. Do not wish to be anything but what you are and try to be that perfectly."

– St. Francis de Sales

Reflection ㉖

....

Uncle Jim's Splendor

> *"So whoever is in Christ is a new creation: the old things have passed away: behold, new things have come." — 2 Corinthians 5:17*

My Uncle Jim was just 51 years old when he died of leukemia. I was 23, but I remember him vividly. My uncle personified "cool." He wore jeans and boots and worked-out before it was popular. He was handsome, with a head of coal black hair and a taut, muscular physique. You name it, Uncle Jim could do it: walk on his hands, water ski, snow ski, dive, swim, hunt, fish, golf. He made the best barbecue ribs in the world and would sneak pieces to me on the side when I was a little girl.

Uncle Jim made me feel special. He genuinely liked me. For an awkward, adolescent girl, being treated well by a guy like Uncle Jim was a wonderful thing.

I remember when he taught me to water ski. I got up on my first attempt, though thinking back, I may have gotten up so quickly to avoid whatever was lurking in that murky water! Regardless, Uncle Jim just kept circling the lake, laughing and yelling, "That a way, Deebs!"

God used my uncle to teach me more than just water skiing. Although Uncle Jim rarely attended church, a year before his death he had a conversion. He was still cool, but now he was a cool guy transformed by the love of Our Lord and His Church. Before he learned of his diagnosis, he humbly said, "If the Lord can love me, He can love anyone."

111

Uncle Jim's conversion influenced me, my mom, and many others, and led us all to a personal relationship with Jesus. Through my uncle, I was introduced to a beautiful group of humble, joy-filled, holy people and I wanted what they had. I wanted what Uncle Jim had. I wanted Jesus. After his death, my uncle's beloved wife, my Aunt Josie, shared with me his last words: "Whatever He wants," he had said.

I'm so grateful for Uncle Jim in my life, and what he taught me about the Lord and about living my splendor. He affirmed who I was when I was young and impressionable, and he drew me to Our Lord by being himself, loving Jesus with his unique personality and sense of humor, and by sharing the story of God's impact on his life. God didn't make Uncle Jim someone else. He doesn't want to make you someone else, either. Rather, He wants to bring you, as He brought my Uncle Jim, into your full splendor, a splendor that has been a part of you since your conception.

Often, we think we have to be "somebody" to make a difference, but the truth is you are somebody the moment you come into existence, the moment the artistic hand of God tenderly brings you into being. You're somebody the moment love enters your heart. You're somebody right now.

You wouldn't be reading this book if God wasn't important in your life. Do you share Him with others? You have loved ones who watch you, learn from you, like I did with my Uncle Jim. Are you making a difference in their lives? Perhaps you're not sure what that even looks like. It looks like you being you, loving Jesus, opening up to others, being honest. Your voice may be the only voice of truth another will ever know.

Today, give thanks for the people in your life who have affirmed your splendor and shared the Lord with you. Ask the Holy Spirit to help you take a small step outside of your comfort zone and share Jesus with another person.

Father God, I praise You and give You glory.
Thank You for those who have loved me,
for those who have formed me in the Faith, for those
You have sent to inspire me.
Please have mercy on them whether they be in this life or the next.
Please Lord, give me the grace and courage
to step out in my world and make a difference in the lives of others.
Please give me the grace to speak with my true voice.
Please give me the courage and opportunity
to share Your life-giving words with others, to make a difference.
Show me this very day.
May I not disappoint You, my Lord.
I love You.
Fill me this day with a greater faith.
Lord, may I have a true conversion.
Blessed Mother, teach me, be with me,
prod me on to do all Our Lord calls me to do.
I rely on you, my Lord and my Lady.
I love you.
Amen.

"*God permits*
everything in view of
a greater
blessing."

– St. Maximilian Kolbe, religious priest
and martyr (age 47), a Polish Conventual
Franciscan friar who volunteered to die in
place of a stranger in the Nazi German
camp of Auschwitz

Reflection ㉗

The Gift of Suffering

"[A]ffliction produces endurance, and endurance, proven character, and proven character hope, and hope does not disappoint...."
— Romans 5:3-5

As I write this, my daughter, Tina, is preparing to move several states away. No longer will I delight in the everyday pleasure of seeing her face and hearing her sweet voice as she kisses me hello and good-bye. God-willing, each of our children grow up and pursue all that they can be. Tina has her own journey, her own splendor to keep discovering and living. And yet...I still cry. My heart aches a bit.

Whether it's the tiny heartaches or the crushing blows, each of us suffers in this life. As my husband Don says, "We all get to take our turn." No matter how hard we attempt to bypass it or speed through heartache, we can't avoid it. In fact, if we use our energy to run away or deny our suffering, there's no opportunity to heal. The Lord calls us to overcome the temptation to speed past our pain. He calls to us in our pain and suffering. As Psalm 34, verse 18, tells us, *"The Lord is close to the brokenhearted; and those who are crushed in spirit He saves."* It's as if our Lord is asking, *Will you trust Me in the small hurts, in the big ones, in bitter times, and in the life-changing moments, trusting that I love you? I will save you. I will bring good out of all of this.*

I'm reminded of two long-suffering, valiant women: One is my beloved Aunt Josie (my Uncle Jim's wife), and the other is my mentor and friend,

Mrs. Ellen, whom I met in my teens over 40 years ago. Both women are widows and both lost adult children who were in the prime of their lives — my aunt lost two daughters and my friend, two sons.

Recently I was blessed to see my Aunt Josie, who is now over 80 years old. She radiated beauty and energy. In the midst of our conversation she encouraged me to "stop pushing" and to be at peace. She assured me that life doesn't have to be crammed into one day. "Honey, there will come another day when you feel like doing what you're struggling with now," she said. Then she added with a sparkle in her eye, "Tonight, have a glass of wine, and, don't be afraid to pour a second."

My dear friend, who is over 90 and so regal in her bearing, never fails to greet me with "How are you honey?" and the question is always so genuine it evokes a response from my heart. Her blue eyes dance and her smile lights up my soul.

Both of these women have unwavering faith and love, and both are a joy to experience. In the midst of much suffering and grief, how have these women managed to exude joy, love, courage, and gratitude? The answer comes from their own lives: They turn into God and not away from Him, hold onto Him, and cling to Him.

Women like my aunt and my friend experience suffering in the arms of their Father. They teach us the transformative power of suffering. They also hold the hand of a familiar friend — that of Our Blessed Mother. On any given day you may see one of them fingering their rosary beads at Mass.

Our Lord gives us His mother as a companion in our suffering. Just as her presence consoled her Son at the foot of the cross, She consoles us. She will hold your hand at the foot of the big crosses, and She deals with the small splinters as well. For me, just holding the Rosary brings great comfort. A few years ago, a distraught mother of a young man killed in a car accident said to me, "I couldn't seem to find the words to pray, and yet, as I held the rosary, I held the hand of the Mother of God and my prayer continued without words."

When life brings suffering, step under the mantle of Our Lady. Just as a child clings to his or her mother for reassurance and love, let Mary enfold you in her mantle of love. Her presence brings comfort and the sweet balm of healing. Bare your soul to Her. She knows suffering and She understands heartache.

Of course, our Lord knows suffering intimately, too. In truth, none of our suffering compares to His at Calvary. If you or a loved one is in the midst of suffering, do not despair — you have company, you have a Lord who understands. Remember that the Resurrection is the other side of Calvary. *Your grief will become joy; you will be sorrowful but your sorrow will turn into joy. —John 16:20*

Believe... Trust... Know that you are not alone...

And remember that your suffering is never in vain. Our Faith teaches us that we can offer our sufferings — big and small — as a prayer.

Today, offer any of your heartaches to the Lord and ask Him to use them to transform you and to help others. And whatever your pain and struggles, ask God, "What are You teaching me? What is it You want me to learn?" And then listen patiently for the answer.

Oh my Lord, you know I hurt.
Please give me the strength to bear my sufferings.
Lord, I'm fragile and yet I can do all things through You, Jesus,
who strengthens me. Be with me, Lord.
Carry me through my trials and through my times of suffering.
Let me not collapse under their weight, but turn to
You for my strength. I need You, Lord.
May my suffering be used for good in my life and in the lives of others.
I pray for a new day when the pain has eased
and joy once again fills my soul.
Only You can do that for me, dear Lord, please help me.
I ask this in Jesus' name.
Amen.

"It is not

the critic who counts; not the man who points out how the strong man stumbles, or where the doer of deeds could have done them better. The credit belongs to the man who is actually in the arena, whose face is marred by dust and sweat and blood; who strives valiantly; who errs, who comes short again and again, because there is no effort without error and shortcoming; but who does actually strive to do the deeds; who knows great enthusiasms, the great devotions; who spends himself in a worthy cause; who at the best knows in the end the triumph of high achievement, and who at the worst, if he fails, at least fails while daring greatly, so that his place shall never be with those cold and timid souls who neither know victory nor defeat."

– Theodore Roosevelt

Reflection 28

"I plead with you — never, ever give up on hope, never doubt, never tire, and never become discouraged. Be not afraid."
— *Pope Saint John Paul II*

In 2011, I attended a conference on healthy living and heard a story that has stayed with me ever since:

During a scientific experiment, insects were placed in a jar with a lid. Initially, the insects flew around inside the jar trying to escape. They would hit the lid at the top, constantly trying to soar higher, but after a while, they got used to the confines of the jar. The researchers wanted to know how the insects would react once the lid was removed so they took it off and, remarkably, the insects kept flying at the same level inside the jar, with no attempt to fly higher and escape.

The researchers also observed that the next generation of insects flew within the same imaginary limits as the previous generation, never once venturing to the space beyond the limits of the lid that no longer existed.

This story made a big impression on me because it's so close to how we humans behave: we get used to what we think are our limits that we never explore what lies beyond them. We can get too comfortable where we are, and never go any further.

Perhaps you, too, have become used to a certain way of being and behaving. There may be limits that you — or others — have placed on your life for so long that it's hard to even recognize them and get past them — you don't even see them. You may have the illusion that you can't go any further than you already are or believe that you can't soar any higher.

Unless you're able to recognize a force operating in your life bigger than yourself, you're settling. That force is bigger than age or illness, bigger than relationship disappointments and loss, bigger than financial challenges, career disappointments, regrets, and resignation.

That force, of course, is God, and living your splendor means growing in freedom and becoming the person He has created you to be, which is about going beyond any false limitations in your life. Begin to notice what these are. A limit that may have been there 10 years ago may not be there any more, or a limit you may think is there may simply be an illusion.

What do you fear to attempt? What continues to resonate in your soul that you repress? How long will you allow fear to have the upper hand? And how long will you stay in a safe, predictable place and never take a risk?

Jesus calls each of us to transformation, not only in our everyday lives, but within our hearts and souls. The call to living your splendor is first and foremost an invitation from God to be, as the best-selling author Mathew Kelley puts it, "the best version of yourself."

A dear friend continues to remind me of her husband's definition of **FEAR** — **F**alse **E**vidence **A**ppearing **R**eal. Jesus invites us to move through our fear and overcome sin in order to enter into holiness and wholeness. To do this we must become aware of any illusions we have about our limitations.

Today, spend some time with the Lord reflecting on the limits you, or others, have placed on your life. Do these free you, or keep you small? Are they even really there? Ask the Lord to help you break through any illusions you have and to expand your horizons so that you may soar to new heights, allowing your splendor to shine ever brighter.

Lord Jesus, You know me.
You know when I sit and when I stand.
You know how I think.
You know my strengths and my weaknesses.
You know me and You love me.
Free me from the shackles that hold me back.
Fill me with newfound energy and life.
I don't want to one day see You, Lord, and regret who I didn't become.
Please, my God, open up my mind, my life.
Please give me the grace to have a positive
mental attitude to try something new
— to think like and be the daughter of the King.
I no longer want to be limited.
I praise You, Lord.
I give You glory.
I believe I'm irreplaceable.
Please give me the drive to take my place in this world!
Amen.

"YOU WILL *Know it*

BY ITS FRUITS; IT WILL CAUSE
YOU TO BE DISCOURAGED,
DOUBTFUL,

CONFUSED."

– From my prayer journal

Reflection ❷❾

. . . .

Overcoming the Evil One's Tactics

> *"Behind the disobedient voice of our first parents lurks a seductive*
> *voice, opposed to God, which makes them fall into death out of*
> *envy. Scripture and the Church's tradition see in this being a fallen*
> *angel, called 'satan' or the 'devil'"*
> — *Catechism of the Catholic Church, 391*

Satan is real. He's the father of lies. He seduces, accuses, and then the final blow: despair. (You may want to remember this by the acronym SAD). The devil wishes to thwart God's work, and sabotage our happiness. A lack of peace is his calling card. He uses various ploys to keep us from living our splendor, to keep the true you from emerging...the holy you. Among other tactics, he uses the "two I's and four D's."

A holy and wise woman explained the "two I's and four D's" to me while helping me discern and work through a tough situation." The two I's stand for Isolation and Inadequacy, and the four D's stand for Disappointment, Discouragement, Doubt, and Despair.

As I was sharing my dilemma, she pointed out that every one of the two I's and four D's were present in my situation. "Wow, that's encouraging!" I thought. And yet in a way, it was good news because I began to see how it was all connected and how I had ended up in a downward spiral...

Even though I have a loving and caring husband and wonderful adult children — as well as a supportive extended family with beloved parents and beautiful friends — I had the sense that I was all alone in the issue that was burdening me. ISOLATION.

Then I had the sense that my work wasn't good enough, I wasn't good enough…. Maybe I just don't have what it takes, I thought. INADEQUACY.
My work wasn't progressing as I'd hoped, so I became DISAPPOINTED. In time, that disappointment turned into further disappointment in other areas of my life…

I became DISCOURAGED. It's not meant to be, I thought. I guess God just doesn't want me to complete this work.

Then DOUBT set in… I began to question whether I'd ever been called to the work in the first place. I doubted my reasons for continuing, and I doubted my motives. I even doubted whether God was listening.

And then came the final blow: DESPAIR. It will never change. I'm relegated to a life of just settling…. Forget my hopes, forget my dreams, they're never going to materialize. Maybe for other folks, but not for me. God uses more talented folks for His work… I'm stuck with the boring stuff. And on and on it went.

What happens as a result of the two I's and the four D's in your life is that communication with God, if not cut off completely, is severely compromised. Anger and resentment set in. Our world becomes small, leaving space for only ourselves. Mental blocks to new ideas, thoughts, and possibilities set in. We justify closing in on ourselves. The real you gets lost, weighted down.

In my situation, once I realized what was happening the downward spiral stopped. I felt like a new person, as if two tons were lifted from my shoulders. All along I had thought this was from God, but once I realized it was just a "ploy" on the part of the devil, I could see my situation with new eyes. Sure my issues remained, but there was a sense of hope about it all. God is with me, He is on my side. He gives me His Mother as she calmly stands with her eyes lifted up to our Lord and her foot on the head of the serpent.

There is great power in knowledge. When you know satan's tools and see them working in your life, you can say, "Not now fella, no way. Get lost. In the name of Jesus I have no time for you!"

For all of us, problems, obstacles, and painful events happen in life, but when we are aware of satan's ploys to tempt us in these moments, we have power to avoid his pitfalls and grasp the hand of God and persevere. As my beloved, Italian grandfather used to say, "When the going gets tough, the tough get going."

So how about you? Any disappointment, discouragement, doubt, or despair in your world? Do you feel Isolated, inadequate, or have you lost hope? Are you weighed down — perhaps by poor health, the loss of a loved one, a sense of emptiness or sadness, financial concerns, family separation, continual worries about children, the loneliness of losing or longing for love? If so, whatever it is, turn your back on the two I's and four D's and give your situation to the Lord. Ask for Our Lady's help, too — her intercession is powerful against satan.

Lord God, I praise You and give You glory.
In the name of Jesus, bless me and heal me.
Remove the blinders from my eyes.
Remove the illusions and the lies of isolation, inadequacy, disappointment,
discouragement, doubt, and despair.
Keep the evil one and his ploys away from me and mine.
In the name of Jesus, please give me the strength to persevere and trust in Your
Word that You will bring good out of all things in my life.
Let me grow in splendor and oneness with You.
Bring forward new life in me and my loved ones each and every day.
I ask all of this in Jesus' name. Amen

"IT'S THE SAME *Jesus* that worked miracles in first century Palestine. He is ready to perform miracles of conversion in our day, provided we believe that He is here with us in the Blessed Sacrament."

— Fr. John Hardon

Reflection ㉚

The Power of Adoration

"Behold I am with you always, until the end of the age."
— Matthew 28:20

Since those days of witnessing the Eucharistic miracle at Lanciano, I have found great solace, rest, and comfort in the presence of the Blessed Sacrament. This is not to say that I don't experience distractions and questions of faith — I do. And yet it doesn't matter, for He is there… my Lord is present to receive me in whatever state I'm in — joy, sadness, confidence, insecurity, confusion, clarity, trust, doubt, in need, or in abundance. He awaits us there; He is present. He understands as no other can. As a holy priest recently shared with me, "Doubts are part and parcel of the human condition and yet the Eucharist is our all in all."

We mustn't be limited by our physical sight. You and I are invited to open our hearts, to see with the eyes of faith. Some of the most profound aspects of our lives are like this. We can't "see" love, yet we believe it exists — we experience it and know it to be real. So too, with the presence of Our Savior who is with us until the end of time.

Our Lord is present to guard His own — and that means you. There's no snatching you out of the Father's hand. The splendor of His Presence is your reminder of His beloved care. It's as if He's saying, *I'm here with you, my daughter. I'm not leaving. I love you. I long to unfold the promise within you, to see your splendor shine in its fullness. You are Mine.*

You are never alone. The evil one wants you to feel isolated, discouraged, and despairing. He wants you to get caught up in chaos where you don't take time to pray, where you are forgetful of the active presence of God in your life. He wants to turn you against yourself. But God calls each one of us to turn towards Him instead. Adoration of the Lord in the Blessed Sacrament helps us to do that.

Pope Saint John Paul II reminded us (in a speech during one of his Apostolic Pilgrimages to Scandinavia in 1989) that: "...when we forget God, we soon lose sight of the deeper meaning of our existence; we no longer know who we are." If you wish to know who you are spend time in Adoration, in the presence of our Lord. Adoration will allow you to fall in love with your Creator. It is through Him that you see your splendor because in His presence, through grace, you are reminded that you are His, that you are a daughter of the King, that you have value. This is our legacy. We are His, made in His image and likeness, and these truths are the foundation of our splendor.

Adoration brings you face to face with the Creator of your soul. How Christ must love you, how He must have anticipated your hurts, your needs, how He must have known your longing for a safe haven. How He must yearn to comfort, to transform, to instill hope, to console, to unfold the splendor you possess... all while being present to you in the Blessed Sacrament.

I remember attending the ordination of a dear and holy friend of one my brothers. This newly ordained priest encouraged us to call upon Our Mother to help us come closer to Jesus in the Blessed Sacrament by saying, "Dear Lady, wrap your divine mantle around us and kiss us with your divine kiss.... Help us to recognize the true presence of Jesus in the Eucharist."

Part of discovering your splendor, of bringing it forward, is to discover the beauty of Jesus in the Blessed Sacrament... to spend time with Him. He's as real to you and to me now as He was to the Apostles almost 2,000 years ago. He's alive! He's waiting... go to Him.

Should you be unable to visit or receive Jesus in the Eucharist, consider making spiritual communions or acts of adoration. You can do this by asking our Lord to enter your heart and soul as if you were physically receiving Him in the Eucharist, or to receive your adoration as if you were physically kneeling before Him. He will bless you for this act of faith. Be assured that He bends to hear you as you pray for the desires of your heart.

Today, take a moment to turn over all the burdens and conflicting emotions to our Lord. If you can, plan a time to visit the Lord in the tabernacle at a nearby church and be with Him there. This God of ours, who allows Himself to be present with you and me always, waits for us, almost as a prisoner of love, in the Blessed Sacrament.

Oh Most Holy Trinity, Father, Son and Holy Spirit,
I adore Thee profoundly.
I offer Thee the most precious Body, Blood, Soul
and Divinity of Jesus Christ present in all the tabernacles of the world,
in reparation for the outrageous sacrileges
and indifference by which He is offended.
By the infinite merits of the Sacred Heart of Jesus
and the Immaculate Heart of Mary,
I beg the conversion of poor sinners.
(Guardian Angel of Fatima, 1916, Act of Reparation to the Holy Trinity)

Promises of the *Devotion of*

the Sacred Heart of Jesus
(as told to St. Margaret Mary Alacoque in 1672):

1. I will give them all the graces necessary in their state of life.

2. I will establish peace in their families.

3. I will comfort them in all their afflictions.

4. I will be their secure refuge during life and above all in death.

5. I will pour abundant blessings on all their undertakings.

6. Sinners shall find in My Heart the source and the infinite ocean of mercy.

7. Tepid souls shall become fervent.

8. Fervent souls shall speedily rise to great perfection.

9. I will bless every place where a picture of My Heart shall be exposed and honored.

10. I will give to priests the gift of touching the most hardened hearts.

11. Those who shall promote this devotion shall have their names written in My Heart, never to be blotted out.

12. The all-powerful love of My Heart will grant to all those who shall receive communion on the first Friday of nine consecutive months the grace of final repentance; they shall not die under my displeasure, nor without receiving their Sacraments; My Divine Heart shall be their safe refuge in this last moment.

Reflection ③

The Man with the Waiting Heart

> *"We all need a 'center' to our lives, a source of truth and goodness from which to draw in the various situations and exertions of daily life. Each of us, when we pause in silence, needs to feel not only the beating of our own heart but, deeper down, the pulsing of a reliable presence, perceptible with the senses of faith, yet real: the presence of Christ, heart of the world."*
> — *Pope Benedict XVI, Angelus, June 2011*

In my childhood home, my parents had an image of the Sacred Heart of Jesus in a prominent place. Initially, I had difficulty relating to the image: A long-haired, bearded man's exposed heart wrapped in thorns. And yet something began to draw my heart closer to this image: the figure of a man quietly bowing in prayer before it every morning and every night when I was growing up. That man — my father — and his silent devotion affected me in ways I wouldn't fully understand until years later.

I look back and realize that observing my dad day after day, year after year, praying before the Sacred Heart touched my soul and taught me what it means to be humble before God, and to begin and end the day before God. Dad taught me volumes without saying a word…

He taught me virtue.
He taught me humility.
He taught me simplicity.
He taught me surrender.

He taught me that he wasn't the center of the universe — God is.

Dad did all this on bended knee.

There is something about this memory that brings me solace, support, and safety. A man who bows before God isn't prideful, arrogant, egotistical, or weak. And now, all grown up, I find a safe harbor in the Sacred Heart of Jesus myself. An image of the Sacred Heart hangs in my home and on many dark nights my husband and I have knelt before it in worry and in hope.

Not too long ago I asked my dad, "Pop, when you pray, how do you pray?" And he said, "Honey, sometimes I don't even know how to express what I'm feeling and I say, 'Good Lord, You know my heart. Take care of everything.'"

The heart speaks its own wisdom and we women seem particularly blessed with a heart that feels deeply and senses what's needed — and that's a good thing. The heart has eyes to see and ears to hear; it has its own voice and its own wisdom.

Jesus in His divinity shared in our humanity — He, too, has a human heart. My dad realized this simple and profound truth and trusted in the love of the Sacred Heart of Jesus. Maybe it's time for you and me to trust more in the heart of Jesus, too — to say, "Good Lord, you know my heart. Take care of everything." Jesus really does know your heart, and He knows even more than you do about your deepest feelings and desires.

Today, remember you are wanted by the Savior of the world. He loves you. He longs to be close to you. He wants to take up residence in your heart. Maybe a first step is for Him to take up residence in your home. Think about placing an image of the Sacred Heart of Jesus in the heart of your home as a reminder of His love. He promises to bless the homes where an image of His Heart is displayed and honored.

Oh most holy Heart of Jesus, fountain of every blessing,
I adore You,
I love You,
and with a lively sorrow for my sins,
I offer You this poor heart of mine.
Make me humble, patient, pure and wholly obedient to Your will.
Grant, good Jesus, that I may live in You and for You.
Protect me in the midst of danger;
comfort me in my afflictions;
give me health of body, assistance in my temporal needs,
Your blessing on all that I do,
and the grace of a holy death.
Amen.
(Prayer to the Sacred Heart of Jesus)

"Hope is

the fragrance of a beloved
soul united with its maker."
— From my prayer journal

Reflection ㉜

· ·

Persevering in Hope

> *"Jesus looked at them and said, 'For human beings this is impossible but for God all things are possible.' " — Matthew 19:26*

All of us can use more hope in our lives. Hope is the fruit of prayer and trust. It's about believing in God's goodness. It's another way to understand perseverance — clinging to God when all seems lost. Hope can mount wings and take you where you never thought possible. It beckons to us, calling us to live our splendor.

Maybe you feel as if you've been relying on God for something, but nothing changes. Perhaps your situation has only gotten worse. How do you persevere in hope, especially when things are difficult?

Some years ago I met a faith-filled, remarkable young woman while working together on some pro-life legislation. At the time, she was 38, and after our time together she became pregnant. A few months later, she miscarried, and that pattern continued for the next seven years with seven miscarriages (including twins).

While my friend and her husband underwent a roller coaster of emotions, their four-year-old daughter continued to pray and hope for another baby. She would say out loud, "Mommy, I pray every day that you will have a baby." And as the years rolled on, this little girl secretly persevered in prayer.

In July of 2013, at the age of 46, my friend was once again pregnant, and once again the problems began as they had so many times before — but this time it was different. The pregnancy continued — and her little one made it! At 46, after eight years of prayer and so many losses, a beautiful baby girl— my god-daughter—entered the world. She's an absolute doll — healthy in every way. And her big sister smiles from ear to ear because she, now 12 years old, knows the power of persevering in hope and never giving up.

Perhaps you've been disappointed one too many times and have a reluctance to grasp hold of hope. But God's love and your tomorrow are not limited by the past. Hope is the smile of the future. As St. Theresa of Avila said, "Pain is never permanent." God calls us to hope always. It is fuel for our splendor, for fruitful living, for abundant life, for miracles.

Hope isn't Pollyannaism, and it isn't optimism either. A pro-life colleague, friend, and author, Jason Jones, wrote:

"Optimism is the fragile dream that pervaded the West in 2001. It was shattered by just one attack. Hope can survive in cancer wards and even concentration camps — as Alexander Solzhenitsyn and Victor Frankl have testified. Hope exists, if you will, in a fourth dimension that cuts across the world we can see at an angle we cannot imagine. It rises from secret places in the heart where the torturers cannot find it, and spreads through quiet gestures and silent prayers they cannot quash." ("From a Clear Blue Sky," Crisis Magazine, October 24, 2011)

God calls us beyond our circumstances into the miraculous. He calls us to leave a space for His hope in our trouble… and that space is prayer. He calls us to persevere and to avoid despair… sharing our pain with others, and with Him. A good one to grab hold of is Our Lady. The Blessed Mother is no stranger to suffering. She knows what it is to persevere and to hope. She'll accompany you through any darkness into the light. She will help you to hold steadfast to the deepest desires of your heart no matter the circumstances you face.

Today, be assured that the God who has experienced all and is above all is with you, and will not leave you orphaned or empty.

Lord God, You know I have a tendency
to be in conflict with myself.
Please silence the inner chatter.
Help me to rely and focus on You rather
than my regrets, my worries.
Lord I trust more in Your hope,
Your power for the miraculous than the
circumstances I face.
Lord, I believe with You all things are possible.
Help my lack of belief. Lord, You know my heart,
take care of everything.
Be with me Jesus.
Amen.

"... *anyone who* had been present then on Mt. Calvary would have seen two altars on which two great sacrifices were being offered: the one in the body of Jesus, the other in the heart of *Mary.*"

— St. John Chrysostom

Reflection 33

Our Lady of Splendor

"Take delight in the Lord, and He will give you the desires of your heart." — Psalm 37:4

My third child, Craig, was conceived in the midst of a 54-day rosary novena that I was praying with my husband and our friend, Sister Mary Rose. When Craig was born, he suffered the same medical affliction as his older sisters; he struggled to breathe and spent his first days of life in the neonatal ICU. Praise God, with expert medical care and the heartfelt prayers of many, our beautiful son survived.

Right after we brought Craig home, however, I was told I couldn't have more children due to a tumor on my pituitary gland. I was only 28 years old. As the eldest of eight from a loving family, my heart's desire had always been to have a large family myself.

As I tried to cope with the death of a dream and worried about my baby boy's ongoing health problems, I picked up my rosary one day and found myself uttering the words, "Blessed Mother, I don't even know what to pray for." At that moment I heard in my heart the gentle words: *Pray for the desires of your heart. Pray for the desires of your heart.*

I began to cry. In light of what I was feeling and what my husband and I faced, I was being given permission to pray for the desires of my heart! It filled me with great consolation and peace.

So, I prayed that Craig would be well and that he and his sister Annie would have brothers and sisters. And within one month of that prayer, I was pregnant — with twins! Little Tina and Toni had the worst medical prognosis of all five of my children — in fact, the priest waited outside the delivery room to immediately baptize them. But as I write this reflection, my little babies are now 30 years old.

The Blessed Mother helped me to honor what was in my heart, and to trust that God would be there for me no matter what happened. This is the gift that Jesus gives us in His Mother, whose splendor is available to all of us through our trials and challenges. She is there for us at every moment of our lives.

Perhaps you know the touch of her loving hand — a hand that gently consoles, reassures, encourages, and makes way. Or maybe you've been reluctant to take a look at her. If so, you're missing out on one of the greatest masterpieces God ever created. Maybe you've never felt the need to draw close to Our Lady, or you think it will take something away from your relationship with Jesus. But, you need not worry that she will crowd out Jesus — to the contrary she'll help you to open your heart more and more to accept His full love and presence.

As the Venerable Archbishop Fulton Sheen once said, "God, who made the sun, also made the moon. The moon does not take away from the brilliance of the sun...All its light is reflected from the sun. The Blessed Mother reflects her Divine Son; without Him, she is nothing. With Him, she is the Mother of Men" (The World's First Love).

Our Lady is our sure pathway to Jesus; a perfect mother, friend, and model of splendor. She knows what it is to surrender, to accept, to persevere, to be happy and sad, to suffer, to love a man, to be a woman. She knows what it is to have an untimely pregnancy and to be lovingly present at the foot of her dying Son's cross.

She knows what it means to surrender and to say yes, even when she didn't understand; to persevere without having it all sorted out; to enjoy and to suffer; to be young and to grow older.

Perhaps it's time to clasp the hand of your mother. Jesus sends her to you as your friend and companion. Today, ask Mary to be that friend to you, and to help you live out your splendor.

Lord, thank You for the gift of Your mother.
Don't let me miss her!
Dear Lady, I long to know you, to draw closer to you.
Be my friend, my comforter, my heavenly mother.
And may I experience the comfort of being one with you, my mother.
I ask this in Jesus' name.
Amen.

"*Stop directing* your life."

Think of a symphony. All the pieces harmonize under the conductor's direction. I am the conductor of your life. Trust in my directive hand."

— From my prayer journal

My Hope

Your journey to splendor continues.

Oftentimes the journeys we make are enhanced by others who travel with us, who accompany us on the way. You may wish to read and discuss *The Splendor of You* with a companion or in a group. If so, discussion questions to *The Splendor of You* can be found by visiting www.SplendorOfYou.com.

Please know that I hold you, dear reader, close to my heart and I pray that our Lord will bless you with insight and grace to become all that He created you to be. It's my fervent hope that in some small way the message of this book has helped you connect to your life source — to the Divine Creator who makes all things new.

I'm so grateful to have been part of your journey to splendor.

May God bless you,

Deby

and together they
danced
and
danced...

Epilogue
....

Once there was a little girl. She danced and loved freely. She had hopes, dreams, possibilities, promise…

She possessed a treasure within her that was only hers; a treasure given to her from a great and wonderful King. Within this treasure was all that made the little girl who she was, unique and matchless. The King told her, "You are my masterpiece–you with your sensitivity, your unique temperament, your love, your gifts, your heart, your singular personality. You are one of a kind and I love you.

The little girl danced with joy for she believed the King.

And then, as time went on… the little girl seemed to dance less and less.

Before she knew it… walls of loss and failure were built around her treasure… walls of sin, fear doubt and hurt. There were even walls of confusion and heartache, walls of disappointment and inadequacy. Some were built by her and some built by others… yet the treasure remained, although it was difficult to see for the walls blocked it from shining through.

Now and then thoughts of the treasure within came to the little girl; but as the years passed on, she hoped for more but she settled for less and less.

One night she found herself thinking about the King's words, you are my masterpiece. She wondered whether her treasure remained. As she called out to the great King, He reassured her that the treasure was still within her and He possessed the key. He went on to tell her that He had been awaiting the moment when she would allow Him to break down the walls surrounding her treasure and let it shine once again.

She cried out, "Please dear King, knock down the walls that block my treasure. Use your key to unlock it!" The King eagerly complied, and with time and urging she began to rediscover her treasure… she began to claim it as her very own!

At times she would question once again, "Am I really a masterpiece?" But having learned to immediately run in haste to her King, she would call out, "Oh my King, help me!" and the dear King would once again gather her in His arms, close to His heart—consoling her and gently reminding her that "all is well," for He was her King and she was His masterpiece.

The treasure grew in brightness and seemed to sparkle more and more. So much so that the little girl, now all grown up, lived out of her treasure… her splendor… her uniqueness… and once again she believed the King. She listened to His whisper of love and tenderness, and together they danced and danced!

Lord,
In this moment, help me to know my needs
and how best to meet them.
May my journey to
splendor continue…

Acknowledgements

There are moments in life when words are inadequate to express the sentiment of the heart. This is such a moment for me, as I humbly thank those who've made this book possible.

God has richly blessed me with family and beloved friends, many of whom are part of *The Splendor of You*®, if not directly then indirectly, for they've given of their heart to me; they've encouraged me, bolstered me, and lifted me up. They've guided me, prodded me, and challenged me to go deeper, to question, and to realize my own splendor. Their all-embracing love has been constant and reminded me that I am the daughter of a great King, the Heavenly Father, beautifully and wonderfully made.

And so first to my mom and dad — thank you for supporting me. You have loved me unconditionally for as long as I can remember, and believed I was capable of reaching my dreams. As a little girl I remember you telling me that I could do anything I wanted…anything. I pray that you are proud of this work and know how much I love you.

To my sister Cindy (Sis); my six brothers —Tony, Jim, Gregg, Buff, Doug, Nick; my five sisters-in-law — Peggy (enjoying heaven), Kathryn, Mary Ann, Susan, Molly; my brother-in-law Dan; and my many nieces and nephews — thank you for believing in me, for encouraging me, for loving me even when I found it tough to love myself. I love you.

To my beloved family and friends who poured over many versions of my manuscript with highlighter in hand, and listened to reflection after reflection, encouraging me along the way. I'm so grateful to those of you who, when life crowded in and I moved away from this work, constantly asked me, "What about your book?" And to those of you who prayed for me — thank you. Without your love and friendship, your input, your reminders, and your cheering me on, this work would never have seen the light of day. You know who you are (best buddy!)… Thank you.

To my Don's "big girls" ~ I love you.

To the many listeners of my Catholic radio show who've tuned in for more than a decade, and the many generous audiences who've encouraged me over the years, giving purpose to *The Splendor of You*® through your smiles, personal stories, emails, and comments — thank you for allowing me to share in your journey.

Early on in the process of writing this book, I had much-appreciated editorial assistance from two talented women — MaryBeth "MB" Rolwes and Mary Ann Sansone. Thank you, both. You took what was a humble work with gaps and flaws, improved it, and encouraged me to keep going. You are dear to my heart. And to life and business coach, Margaret Fortner — thank you for your support and encouragement early on in this process (and thanks to your dear mom). Honey, working with you was and is pure gift.

A special thanks also to Mac Moore for his legal acumen and endless patience.

To my editor Zoe Romanowsky — thank you for your creativity, keen insight, stellar intellect, professional experience, and for keeping me on task. Zoe, it took three years to have the opportunity to work with you, but it was well worth the wait! And a big thank you to Christina Jopson & my Annie who lent their proof-reading expertise to this work.

To the talented and encouraging John Caurso (special thanks to Annie and her buddies Susie and Ashok) - Thank you for your beautiful book cover design and professional expertise. Your guidance has been invaluable. And to the creative and artistic master Jim Harper (thanks Jimmy Jr. & your mom!), enthusiastic from the onset, who designed and laid out this book, and to Jane Tayon, who shepherded this work all the way to its printing with her matchless energy and spirit ("I got this one!") — thank you. A special thanks to Tony Taylor for his encouragement and for generously sharing his time and extraordinary talent. Your calm, kind manner kept me in check on more than one occasion! And to dear Jen Singleton who's extraordinary creative skills brought this work across the finish line.

To Dr. Richard Johnson, who from the beginning gave me the confidence to go the distance. You formatted, encouraged, read change after change, directed, guided, coached, counseled, and gently pushed me year after year as life's circumstances prompted me to shelve this work time and time again. Thank you, Dr. Johnson. More than four years ago while I was praying, anticipating a new year and hoping for new beginnings, I asked the Lord for the next step and it was clear — "continue your work with Dr. Johnson." How grateful I am to have followed that simple and blessed directive.

To the many priests and religious sisters who've guided me in my faith life, particularly Bishop Robert J. Hermann, Msgr. Eugene Morris, Msgr. Henry Breier, Msgr. John Leykam, and Rev. Anthony Ochoa. And to Raymond Cardinal Burke, Timothy Cardinal Dolan, Archbishop Joseph Naumann, Mother Angelina Finnell, D.C.J., Sr. Regina Marie Gorman, O.C.D., Sr. Joseph Andrew Bogdanowicz, O.P., Dr. Mary Fitzgibbons, Teresa Holman, Dr. Ann

Martin, Susanna Pinto, and Patty Schneier — my heartfelt thanks to you all for your support and endorsement. You have deeply honored and blessed me. Each of you has inspired and taught me; I'm grateful beyond words.

To those who have gone on, who deeply inspired this work -- my beloved Sr. Mary Rose, my fun and awesome Uncle Jim, and my beautiful baby Cindi.

And now to my husband and children -- Don, Annie, Cindi, Craig, Tina, Toni. How do I begin to describe what I hold in the depths of my heart for each of you? To Donny — my best friend, my forever love -- thank you. You've had my back from the beginning. You truly know the many moments of struggle when I asked, "Why am I doing this?" and the moments of exasperation when I feared it wasn't good enough; the late nights of reading and re-reading and your countless notes written in the margins of draft after draft. What would I do without you? I love you, honey. Thank you for this moment, the past 36 years, and the hope of new tomorrows. Thank you for believing in me and for believing in *The Splendor of You*®.

To my Annie, my Craigey, my Tina, my Toni — thank you for being my greatest accomplishment and my dream team. You were my support, focus group, researchers, proofreaders, promoters, task masters, and delegators. You, along with your sister, Cindi, and your beautiful daddy, are the answers to the desires of my heart.

An extra special word of thanks to my Toni — honey, thank you for leading this work across the finish line. Without your direction and organizational ability these last few months, coupled with your lawyerly attention to details, your bright mind, your deep faith, your personal belief in this work, there wouldn't be *The Splendor of You*®. Thank you for sharing your much sought-after time and energy to partner with me in completing this book. Sweetheart, I love you and will never forget your gift of self these many months, and our time together.

In closing, I give all glory and honor and thanks to Our Lord and Our Lady. May the Spirit of God fill your heart, dear reader, and may you find comfort and transformative peace in your splendor.

Resources

I have found many inspiring resources over the years to help me deepen my faith and begin to live out my splendor. The following is a list of some of my personal favorites...
See what you think!

Books

A People of Hope: The Challenges Facing the Catholic Church and the Faith That Can Save It, by John L. Allen, Jr. and Cardinal Timothy M. Dolan

As Bread That is Broken by Peter G. van Breemen

Boundaries: When to Say Yes, How to Say No to Take Control of Your Life, by Dr. Henry Cloud and Dr. John Townsend

Captivating by John Eldredge, Stasi Eldredge

Commit Emotional Suicide by Gregory Sansone (Addiction and Recovery)

Discover Your Spiritual Strengths: Find Health, Healing, and Happiness, by Dr. Richard P. Johnson *page 61 (Spiritualstrengthsprofile.com)

Even Better after 50: How to Become (and Remain) Well of Body, Wise of Mind, and Whole of Spirit in the Second Half of Your Life, by Dr. Richard P. Johnson

For a Greater Purpose: Zip Rzeppa - My Life Journey, by Zip Rzeppa

Good to Great: Why Some Companies Make the Leap...and Others Don't, by Jim Collins

Having a Mary Heart in a Martha World: Finding Intimacy with God in the Busyness of Life, by Joanna Weaver

Interior Freedom, by Fr. Jacques Philippe

Into Your Hands, Father: Abandoning Ourselves to the God Who Loves Us, by Fr. Wilfred Stinissen

Left to Tell: Discovering God amidst the Rwandan Holocaust, by Immaculee Ilibagiza

Man's Search for Meaning, by Viktor E. Frankl

One Thousand Gifts: A Dare to Live Fully Right Where You Are, by Ann Voskamp

On Fire: the 7 Choices to Ignite a Radically Inspired Life, by John O'Leary

Ordinary Grace: Daily Gospel Reflections, by the Daughters of St. Paul

Pure Faith: Book of Prayer, by Jason Evert

Recareer: Find Your Authentic Work, by Dr. Richard P. Johnson

Rediscovering Catholicism, Journeying Toward our Spiritual North Star, by Matthew Kelly

Searching for and Maintaining Peace: A Small Treatise on Peace of Heart, by Fr. Jacques Philippe

7 Secrets of Confession, by Vinny Flynn

The Fulfillment of All Desire, by Ralph Martin

The Pocket Therapist: An Emotional Swvival Kit, by Therese J. Borchard

The Race to Save Our Century: Five Core Principles to Promote Peace, Freedom and a Culture of Life, by Jason Scott Jones & John Zmirak

The Rhythm of Life, Living Every Day with Passion & Purpose, by Matthew Kelly

33 Days to Morning Glory: A Do-It-Yourself Retreat in Preparation tor Marian Consecration, by Fr. Michael E. Gaitley, MIC

Transitions: Making Sense of Life's Changes, by William Bridges

True Radiance: Finding Grace in the Second Half of Life, by Lisa Mladinich

Woman First, Family Always, by Kathryn Sansone

Audio

Discernment of Spirits, Fr. James Mason

Heart to Heart: Meditations on Living in the Presence of One Who Loves You, The Letters of Mother Luisita - Carmelite Sisters of the Most Sacred Heart of Los Angeles

The Rosary, by Dana and Fr. Kevin Scallon

DVD

Catholicism, Rev. Robert E. Barron

The Holy Winding Sheet, by Chuck Neff

Music

His Love Remains, Collin Raye

I'm Not Alone, Kim Kalman

Let the Door Swing Wide, Kim Kalman

Sacred Arias, Andrea Bocelli

Mater Eucharistiae - Dominican Sisters of Mary, Mother of the Eucharist

Surrender - Karen Money

Resources continued

....

Examen

It is recommended that you practice doing examen, at least twice a day. This is not an intellectual exercise. It is a prayer. Do not feel compelled to use the same words I happen to use here unless they are helpful. In the beginning, they may be helpful, but as you become comfortable, use your own words.

"How gentle and loving is Your awakening, O Bridegroom Word, in the center and depth of my soul... Awaken and enlighten me, my Lord, so I might know and love the blessings You ever propose to me, and I might understand that you have moved to bestow favors on me and have remembered me." - *St John of the Cross, Living Flame 4:3,9*

THANKSGIVING:
Father, I rejoice in Your love for me. You thought of me and so loved the idea of me that You created me. Each moment You are at work, loving me into existence. Thank You, Father for accepting me as I am. (Here, I thank God for any special gifts I received this particular day e.g. the weather, a good book, a holy desire, a good joke, the ability to hear His voice and/or see Him working . . .etc.)

PETITION
Father, You know me better than I know myself. Please help me be aware of how You worked in and around me today. I wish to respond to Your call for me, with obedience and love. However, for me to follow Your will, I first need to know it. Please help me listen and hear the voice of Your Spirit in me that I may see how You see me.

REFLECTION
In this section you ask yourself some questions as you go through the previous few hours since your last examen. You think of the answers as you are guided by the Spirit.
An example of these questions could be as follows:
1. How am I feeling right now? Why?
2. Is this leading me to God or away from God?
3. How did God manifest His love for me in the last few hours?
4. How did I respond? Was there anything lacking?
5. What did I do to show my love for God?

CONTRITION
Father, thank You for Your care and guidance in the last few hours. I am sorry for the ways in which I was not sensitive to Your Spirit in me. I love You, Lord, and You know where and how I need healing and forgiveness. I surrender myself to You completely (Here one is to be specific as well).

TOGETHER LOOKING TO THE FUTURE

Father with hope I look to the future. You accept me the way I am and You allow me to grow. You give me time and grace, opportunity and space. I place the time between now and my next examen in your hands. I ask you to make me more sensitive to Your Spirit in me. May my life between now and then be united to the life of Your Son, my Lord and Savior, Jesus (Here one is to be specific as well: What is in the coming hours I want to discuss with the Lord, to lift up in prayer, . . . etc.).

As I go forward with You, Lord,
please "strengthen the quiet voice of my conscience,
your own voice, in my life.
Look at me as you looked at Peter.
Let your gaze penetrate my heart
and indicate the direction
my life must take…
Grant me, ever anew,
the grace of conversion."

(Adapted from Cardinal Joseph Ratzinger, *Way of the Cross*, 2005 Carmelite Sisters of the Most Sacred Heart of Los Angeles, 920 East Alhambra Road, Alhambra, CA 91801, (626) 289-1353 www.carmelitesistersocd.com)

✝

*S*PLENDOR OF *Y*OU® COMMUNICATIONS